WINSOR PILATES

Low-Carb Cookbook

Mari Winsor

Publications International, Ltd.

www.pilbooks.com

Pictured on the front cover: Pork Kabobs in Margarita Marinade *(page 124)*.

Pictured on the back cover: Marinated Tomato Salad *(page 162)*, Roasted Chicken with Peppers *(page 110)*, Speedy Pineapple-Lime Sorbet *(page 184)*.

Nutritional Analysis: Nutritional information is given for the recipes in this publication. Each analysis is based on the food items in the ingredient list, except ingredients labeled as "optional" or "for garnish." When more than one ingredient choice is listed, the first ingredient is used for analysis. If a range for the amount of an ingredient is given, the nutritional analysis is based on the lowest amount. Foods offered as "serve with" suggestions are not included in the analysis unless otherwise stated.

Manufactured in China.

Microwave Cooking: Microwave ovens vary in wattage. Use the cooking times as guidelines and check for doneness before adding more time.

54

Introduction   5

Workout
Introduction   10

Nutrient Counter   12

Breakfast   54

Appetizers   72

72

90

CONTENTS

CONTENTS

Soups   90

Main Dishes   110

Sides   142

Desserts   168

Index   189

112

142

172

THE BASICS

The food we eat provides the body with the fuel it needs to function. The blend of fuel we add to our bodies, the amount of fuel we add, and when we add it impacts our long-term health. To fully understand the impact food has on our bodies, let's review some basics.

Food contains calories, which is the measurement of the food's energy potential. All food is composed of three major components: protein, carbohydrate, and fat. These are called macronutrients. Each causes different and complex metabolic reactions in the body.

Protein

Protein is found in all foods, in varying quantities. Animal-based foods such as dairy products, meat, fish, and poultry are the most common source of protein, but plant sources such as beans and tofu also are rich in this vital nutrient. Protein builds and repairs our bodies and helps us access stored energy, which can be a benefit when it comes to maintaining a healthy weight. Protein deficiencies are rare, but they can be debilitating, resulting in a weakened immune system and loss of muscle mass. Consuming too much protein, especially from animal sources, can have negative health implications as well, such as raised blood lipids or fats such as cholesterol.

Good sources of protein include fish, chicken and turkey trimmed of skin and visible fat, lean meats, low-fat dairy products, soyfoods, and beans. Vegetarians can get their protein from nuts, legumes, and all beans, including soyfoods such as tofu, tempeh, and soymilk. Ovo-lacto vegetarians can add eggs and dairy products.

Carbohydrate

Like protein, carbohydrates, sometimes called starches or sugars, are present in all foods in varying amounts. Plant-based foods such as grains, fruits, and vegetables are the most common source of carbohydrates, although some animal-based foods also contain carbs. (Milk, for example, contains lactose, a naturally occurring sugar.) Carbohydrates are the body's primary and preferred source of energy. Once eaten, carbohydrates are converted by our bodies into blood glucose, or blood sugar. Without adequate carbohydrate in our diets, blood sugars can drop too low, causing a condition known as hypoglycemia. Symptoms include nervousness, anxiety, sweating, and food cravings. It is important for successful weight management and for health concerns such as diabetes to control carbohydrate intake to keep blood sugar levels from spiking too high or dipping too low. Fluctuating blood sugars and food cravings triggered by an energy-starved brain can easily derail the most determined dieter.

However, all carbohydrates are not created equal. Some carbohydrates are better than others because they are metabolized by the body more slowly, which helps avoid blood sugar highs and lows. Mother Nature has provide us with two types of carbs—**simple** and **complex**—and modern man has created a third, **refined carbohydrates.** Simple carbohydrates such as table sugar have no fiber and are quickly absorbed into the bloodstream; refined carbohydrates—including white bread, many children's breakfast cereals, pasta, and white rice—have had much or all of their natural fiber and bran milled away, and also enter the bloodstream relatively quickly. The trick is to eat "good" carbs: complex carbohydrates. Complex carbohydrates such as whole grains or beans, retain their natural fiber and bran, which helps slow the absorption of glucose into the bloodstream.

How much carbohydrate foods contain and how quickly that carbohydrate is converted to blood glucose and enters the bloodstream is measured on scale called the **glycemic index.** Complex carbohydrates have lower (meaning better) ratings on the glycemic index than highly refined or simple carbohydrates, which have higher ratings. The speed at which carbohydrates are converted and enter the bloodstream is important because it determines how much of the hormone **insulin** will be produced. Insulin is produced by the pancreas, a large gland that also discharges enzymes into the intestine. Insulin's job is to store fat and bring nutrients into cells.

The importance of **fiber** in helping to regulate blood glucose should not be under-estimated. Eating an orange is better than drinking orange juice because the fiber in the orange slows the uptake of the sugar. Even though fiber is indigestible, it plays an important role in weight loss because it's the "slow down" sign in the road for the absorption of carbohydrates. The higher the fiber content of the carbohydrate, the slower the sugars derived from the carbohydrate enter the bloodstream. Since most of us don't eat just one food at a time, the glycemic index has limited value when it comes to real life and everyday eating. When you eat sensibly—lean protein, beneficial fats, and whole, high-fiber carbohydrates—you've eaten in a balanced way. It's as simple as that.

Fat

The most misunderstood macronutrient is fat. Fats have gotten a bad rap for more than 20 years. Misinformation about fat is responsible for much of the obesity and disease prevalent in the country today. The truth is, it takes fat to burn fat. That is, it takes dietary fat to burn body fat. We need to take in fat from the foods we eat. Fat-containing foods supply us with **essential fatty acids,** and "EFAs" play an important role in a properly functioning immune system, in supplying energy, in balancing hormones, in keeping blood sugar levels stabilized, and, finally, in controlling hunger.

We've all heard about "good" fats and "bad" fats. Fats are derived from both animal and plant sources, and there are three different types: **saturated, polyunsaturated,** and

monounsaturated fats. Unfortunately, scientists don't always agree as to what exact percentage of which fat constitutes the "ultimate" healthful diet. However, medical studies do show there are health benefits from eating greater amounts of the monounsaturated fats that come from olive oil, macadamia nuts, and avocados. And all studies do agree that highly processed fats—called hydrogenated or partially hydrogenated, such as margarine and shortening—are detrimental to health. These trans-fatty acids contribute to disease in much the same way saturated animal fats do: by elevating blood lipids and cholesterol.

Fats are responsible for causing the release of an important hormone, **cholecys-tokinin,** or CCK for short. CCK turns off the hunger switch—a very important factor in dieting! CCK signals your brain when you are full and need to stop eating. Fat also adds flavor to food and makes it taste good. Think of the difference between ices and ice cream. It's the fat that adds the "texture" to foods. And even more important is the fact that fats slow down the rate of absorption of sugar into the bloodstream.

In the absence of adequate fat and protein, the body is forced to recruit these vital nutrients by breaking down its own muscle and bone mass. It becomes a vicious cycle, because less muscle mass leads to greater fat storage. Remember, anything that slows the uptake of insulin, the fat-storage hormone, is an aid to weight loss. So don't be afraid to eat fats. Just choose the good ones like olive oil, avocados, fish and fish oils, and fats from nuts, especially macadamia nuts.

The Right Combination

All popular diet plans rely on restricting calories by "adjusting" the amount of protein, carbohydrates, and fats we eat. A sensible eating plan relies less on the caloric approach and more on the way the foods we eat are handled by the body. Why? Because this approach keeps insulin in check and controls your hormonal responses to the foods you eat. When each meal and snack has the proper amount of lean protein, high-fiber complex carbohydrates, and beneficial fats, the results can be astounding. Not only should you find it easier to lose fat, but you should feel full after each meal and be free from the craving that is so problematic in many other diets.

The complex relationship that exists between body fat, the foods we eat, and insulin and blood sugar can be summed up in a simple concept: If you eat too many refined or simple carbohydrates, your body will produce high levels of insulin—a fat-storage hormone—and you will gain weight. The answer is not in eliminating carbohydrates, but in eating the high-fiber carbohydrates, along with lean protein and beneficial fats.

Simple Steps to Weight Loss

1. Never go more than five hours without eating. This will keep you in proper hormonal balance.
2. Drink lots of water. You'll need it to break down fat and flush out toxins.
3. Don't drink soda or beverages containing caffeine.
4. Don't drink juices—always eat the fruit instead.
5. Eat breakfast within one hour of rising.
6. Eat your first snack between lunch and dinner.
7. Eat your second snack an hour before going to bed.
8. Remember to keep movement and exercise as part of your lifestyle.

Following these simple steps may lead you to living a healthier lifestyle and attaining your weight loss goals and higher levels of health. Good luck!

EXERCISES

1 The ROLL-UP

Position

Lie flat on your back. Your spine is against the floor. Reach your arms above your head.

Action

Breathe in and raise your arms toward the ceiling. Use the powerhouse to bring your chin into your chest. Reach through your fingertips. Exhale as you continue reaching with your arms, curling over as your fingers reach toward your toes. Create a "C" curve in your lower back. Then slowly roll back. Repeat 6 to 8 times.

Basic TRAINING TIPS

1 Always drink plenty of water. Hydrating the body is nature's first defense.

2 Consistency is the name of the game. Keep your routine going.

3 Maintain your diet.

4 It's okay to take a day off.

5 Be creative. If there's not enough space in your room, use the hotel gym, or even the bed.

2 Single Leg STRETCH

Position

Lie flat on your back. Your arms rest against your body. Inhale slowly and lift your chin toward your chest.

Action

Use your powerhouse to raise your head and shoulders off the mat. At the same time, bring your right knee into your chest and put your right hand on your right ankle, while your left hand is placed atop the inside of your right knee. Relax your shoulders and open your elbows. Relax your ankle. Tug on the bent leg twice, breathing out as you go. Switch legs. Left hand to left ankle, right hand atop the inside of your left knee. Tug twice and switch. Repeat 8 to 12 times.

3 Little Bit of HEAVEN

Position

You are lying on your stomach.

Action

Use your hands and arms to push yourself back onto your heels until you are kneeling with your back rounded over. Focus on the mat. Extend your arms long in front of you. Push your hips to your heels for a deep lower-back stretch. Breathe slowly and deeply. Rest the back.

THE NUTRIENT COUNTER

Sticking to a low-carb diet means you have to choose your carbs carefully. But it can be hard to distinguish foods that are high in carbs from those that aren't.

This nutrient counter will help you separate high-carb foods from low-carb foods. The counter lists the calories and the number of grams of total carbohydrate, fiber, protein, total fat, and saturated fat in a portion. (Fiber is included in the number of grams of total carbohydrate, but the number of fiber grams is broken out so you can see how many of a food's carb grams come from this indigestible nutrient.)

Values have been rounded to the nearest whole number. "Tr" (for trace) means there's less than half a gram of that nutrient in a single portion; "na" means the value was not available. If you eat a higher-carb meal, use the counter to help you choose foods that will get you back on track.

Food, portion	Cal	Total Carb (g)	Fiber (g)	Protein (g)	Total Fat (g)	Sat Fat (g)
BAKED PRODUCTS						
Bagel (includes plain, onion, poppy, sesame), 1 medium	289	56	2	11	2	Tr
Biscuits, plain or buttermilk, 1 medium	186	25	1	3	8	1
Bread, cornbread, made with low-fat (2%) milk, 1 piece	173	28	na	4	5	1
Bread, French or Vienna (includes sourdough), 1 slice, medium	175	33	2	6	2	Tr
Bread, Italian, 1 slice, medium	54	10	1	2	1	Tr

Food, portion	Cal	Total Carb (g)	Fiber (g)	Protein (g)	Total Fat (g)	Sat Fat (g)
BAKED PRODUCTS *(CONT.)*						
Bread, pita, white, 1 small	77	16	1	3	Tr	Tr
Bread, white, 1 slice	67	13	1	2	1	Tr
Bread, whole-wheat, 1 slice	69	13	2	3	1	Tr
Brownies, 1 large square	227	36	1	3	9	2
Cake, chocolate, without frosting, 1/12 of 9" dia	340	51	2	5	14	5
Cake, pound, 1/12 of 12 oz	109	14	Tr	2	6	3
Cake, yellow, 1/12 of 8" dia	245	36	Tr	4	10	3
Cheesecake, 1/6 of 17 oz	257	20	Tr	4	18	8
Cookies, butter, 1 cookie	23	3	Tr	Tr	1	1
Cookies, chocolate chip, 1 medium cookie	48	7	Tr	1	2	1
Cookies, sugar, 1 cookie	66	8	Tr	1	3	1

Food, portion	Cal	Total Carb (g)	Fiber (g)	Protein (g)	Total Fat (g)	Sat Fat (g)
Cookies, sugar wafers with creme filling, 1 small wafer	18	2	Tr	Tr	1	Tr
Crackers, cheese, 1 cracker (1" square)	5	1	Tr	Tr	Tr	Tr
Crackers, matzo, plain, 1 matzo	111	23	1	3	Tr	Tr
Crackers, saltines, 1 cracker	13	2	Tr	Tr	Tr	Tr
Crackers, whole-wheat, 1 cracker	18	3	Tr	Tr	1	Tr
Croissants, butter, 1 croissant	231	26	1	5	12	7
Croutons, fast food, 1 package	47	6	1	1	2	1
Danish pastry, fruit, 1 pastry	263	34	1	4	13	3
Doughnuts (cake, plain, frosted, or chocolate-coated), 1 doughnut	204	21	1	2	13	3
English muffins, plain, enriched (includes sourdough), 1 muffin	134	26	2	4	1	Tr
French toast, made with low-fat (2%) milk, 1 slice	149	16	na	5	7	2

Food, portion	Cal	Total Carb (g)	Fiber (g)	Protein (g)	Total Fat (g)	Sat Fat (g)
BAKED PRODUCTS *(CONT.)*						
Graham crackers, 2½" square	30	5	Tr	Tr	1	Tr
Muffins, blueberry, 1 medium	313	54	3	6	7	2
Pancakes, 1 pancake (4" dia)	74	14	Tr	2	1	Tr
Pie, apple, ⅙ of 8" dia	277	40	2	2	13	4
Pie, pecan, ⅛ of 9" dia	503	64	na	6	27	5
Rolls, dinner, plain, 1 roll	84	14	1	2	2	Tr
Rolls, burger or hot dog, 1 roll	120	21	1	4	2	Tr
Rolls, hard, 1 roll	167	30	1	6	2	Tr
Sweet rolls, cinnamon, with raisins, 1 roll	223	31	1	4	10	2
Taco shells, baked, 1 medium	62	8	1	1	3	Tr
Tortillas, corn, 1 tortilla	53	11	1	1	1	Tr

Food, portion	Cal	Total Carb (g)	Fiber (g)	Protein (g)	Total Fat (g)	Sat Fat (g)
Tortillas, flour, 1 tortilla	150	26	2	4	3	1
Waffles, plain, frozen, ready-to-heat, 1 waffle square	98	15	1	2	3	1

BEEF PRODUCTS

Food, portion	Cal	Total Carb (g)	Fiber (g)	Protein (g)	Total Fat (g)	Sat Fat (g)
Beef, ground, 85% lean/15% fat, broiled, 1 patty (¼ lb raw)	193	0	0	20	12	5
Bottom round, braised, 3 oz	234	0	0	24	14	5
Brisket, whole, braised, 3 oz	327	0	0	20	27	11
Chuck, arm roast, braised, 3 oz	282	0	0	23	20	8
Corned beef, brisket, cured, cooked, 3 oz	213	Tr	0	15	16	5
Eye of round, roasted, 3 oz	195	0	0	23	11	4
Liver, pan-fried, 1 slice	142	4	0	21	4	1
Rib, prime, roasted, 3 oz	361	0	0	18	31	13

Food, portion	Cal	Total Carb (g)	Fiber (g)	Protein (g)	Total Fat (g)	Sat Fat (g)
BEEF PRODUCTS *(CONT.)*						
Skirt steak, broiled, 3 oz	174	0	0	23	9	3
Top sirloin, broiled, 3 oz	219	0	0	24	13	5
BEVERAGES						
Beer, regular, 12 fl oz	117	6	Tr	1	Tr	0
Carbonated beverage, low-calorie, other than cola or pepper, with aspartame, 12 fl oz	0	0	0	Tr	0	0
Citrus fruit juice drink, frozen concentrate, prepared with water, 8 fl oz	124	30	Tr	Tr	Tr	0
Club soda, 12 fl oz	0	0	0	0	0	0
Cocoa mix, powder, 3 heaping tsp	111	24	1	2	1	1
Coffee, brewed from grounds, 8 fl oz	9	0	0	Tr	2	0
Cola, carbonated, 12 fl oz	155	40	0	Tr	0	0

NUTRIENT COUNTER

Food, portion	Cal	Total Carb (g)	Fiber (g)	Protein (g)	Total Fat (g)	Sat Fat (g)
Cola, carbonated, low-calorie, with aspartame, 12 fl oz	4	Tr	0	Tr	0	0
Cranberry-apple juice drink, 8 fl oz	174	44	Tr	Tr	Tr	0
Fruit punch drink, frozen concentrate, prepared, 8 fl oz	114	29	Tr	Tr	0	Tr
Ginger ale, 12 fl oz	124	32	0	0	0	0
Grape juice drink, 8 fl oz	125	32	na	Tr	0	0
Hard liquor (gin, rum, vodka, whiskey), distilled, 80 proof, 1 jigger (1.5 fl oz)	97	0	0	0	0	0
Lemonade, frozen concentrate, prepared, 8 fl oz	131	34	Tr	Tr	Tr	Tr
Tea, brewed, 8 fl oz	2	1	0	0	0	Tr
Tonic water, 12 fl oz	124	32	na	0	0	0
Wine, dessert, sweet, 3.5 fl oz	165	14	0	Tr	0	0
Wine, table, 3.5 fl oz	79	3	0	Tr	0	0

Food, portion	Cal	Total Carb (g)	Fiber (g)	Protein (g)	Total Fat (g)	Sat Fat (g)
BREAKFAST CEREALS						
ALL-BRAN Original, ½ cup	78	22	10	4	1	Tr
CHEERIOS, 1 cup	111	22	3	3	2	Tr
Corn CHEX, 1 cup	112	26	1	2	Tr	Tr
Corn grits, white, cooked with water, 1 cup	143	31	1	3	Tr	Tr
CREAM OF WHEAT, regular, cooked with water, 1 cup	126	27	1	4	Tr	Tr
Farina, enriched, cooked with water, ¾ cup	84	18	1	2	Tr	Tr
HONEY BUNCHES OF OATS, ¾ cup	118	25	1	2	2	Tr
KELLOGG'S Corn Flakes, 1 cup	101	24	1	2	Tr	Tr
KELLOGG'S Raisin Bran, 1 cup	195	47	7	5	2	Tr
Oats, instant, plain, prepared with water, cooked, 1 cup	129	22	4	5	2	Tr

NUTRIENT COUNTER

Food, portion	Cal	Total Carb (g)	Fiber (g)	Protein (g)	Total Fat (g)	Sat Fat (g)
PRODUCT 19, 1 cup	100	25	1	2	Tr	Tr
QUAKER Low Fat 100% Natural Granola with Raisins, ½ cup	195	41	3	4	3	1
RICE KRISPIES, 1¼ cups	119	29	Tr	2	Tr	Tr
SPECIAL K, 1 cup	117	22	1	7	Tr	Tr

NUTRIENT COUNTER

Food, portion	Cal	Total Carb (g)	Fiber (g)	Protein (g)	Total Fat (g)	Sat Fat (g)
BREAKFAST CEREALS *(CONT.)*						
Wheat germ, toasted, 1 cup	432	56	17	33	12	2
WHEATIES, 1 cup	107	24	3	3	1	Tr
Whole Grain TOTAL, ¾ cup	97	23	2	2	1	Tr
CEREAL GRAINS AND PASTA						
Barley, pearled, cooked, 1 cup	193	44	6	4	1	Tr
Bulgur, cooked, 1 cup	151	34	8	6	Tr	Tr
Corn flour, whole-grain, yellow, 1 cup	422	90	16	8	5	1
Couscous, cooked, 1 cup	176	36	2	6	Tr	Tr
Hominy, canned, white, 1 cup	119	24	4	2	1	Tr
Macaroni, cooked, enriched, 1 cup elbow-shaped	197	40	2	7	1	Tr
Noodles, chow mein, 1 cup	237	26	2	4	14	2

Food, portion	Cal	Total Carb (g)	Fiber (g)	Protein (g)	Total Fat (g)	Sat Fat (g)
Noodles, egg, cooked, 1 cup	213	40	2	8	2	Tr
Noodles, soba, cooked, 1 cup	113	24	na	6	Tr	Tr
Oats, 1 cup	607	103	17	26	11	2
Rice, brown, long-grain, cooked, 1 cup	216	45	4	5	2	Tr
Rice, white, long-grain, cooked, 1 cup	205	45	1	4	Tr	Tr
Spaghetti, cooked, 1 cup	197	40	2	7	1	Tr
Wheat flour, white, bread, enriched, 1 cup	495	99	3	16	2	Tr
Wheat flour, whole-grain, 1 cup	407	87	15	16	2	Tr
Wild rice, cooked, 1 cup	166	35	3	7	1	Tr

DAIRY PRODUCTS

Food, portion	Cal	Total Carb (g)	Fiber (g)	Protein (g)	Total Fat (g)	Sat Fat (g)
Cheese, Brie, 1 oz	95	Tr	0	6	8	5
Cheese, Cheddar, 1 oz	114	Tr	0	7	9	6

Food, portion	Cal	Total Carb (g)	Fiber (g)	Protein (g)	Total Fat (g)	Sat Fat (g)
Dairy Products *(cont.)*						
Cheese, cottage, low-fat, 2% milkfat, 1 cup (not packed)	203	8	0	31	4	3
Cheese, cream, 1 tbsp	51	Tr	0	1	5	3
Cheese, feta, crumbled, 1 cup	396	6	0	21	32	22
Cheese, low-fat, cheddar or Colby, 1 oz	49	1	0	7	2	1
Cheese, mozzarella, part skim, 1 oz	72	1	0	7	5	3
Cheese, ricotta, part skim, ½ cup	171	6	0	14	10	6
Cheese, Swiss, 1 oz	108	2	0	8	8	5
Cheese food, pasteurized process, American, 1 oz	94	2	0	5	7	4
Cream, half-and-half, 1 tbsp	20	1	0	Tr	2	1
Cream, heavy whipping, 1 cup, whipped	414	3	0	2	44	28

Food, portion	Cal	Total Carb (g)	Fiber (g)	Protein (g)	Total Fat (g)	Sat Fat (g)
Cream, light (coffee or table), 1 individual container	22	Tr	0	Tr	2	1
Cream, sour, 1 tbsp	26	1	0	Tr	3	2
Cream, whipped, topping, pressurized, 1 tbsp	8	Tr	0	Tr	1	Tr
Egg, whole, hard-boiled, chopped, 1 cup	211	2	0	17	14	4
Egg, whole, raw, fresh, 1 large	74	Tr	0	6	5	2
Egg, whole, scrambled, 1 large	101	1	0	7	7	2
Egg substitute, liquid, 1 cup	211	2	0	30	8	2
Milk, 2%, 1 cup	122	11	0	8	5	2
Milk, buttermilk, low-fat, 1 cup	98	12	0	8	2	1
Milk, canned, condensed, sweetened, 1 cup	982	166	0	24	27	17
Milk, canned, evaporated, 1 cup	338	25	0	17	19	12

NUTRIENT COUNTER

Food, portion	Cal	Total Carb (g)	Fiber (g)	Protein (g)	Total Fat (g)	Sat Fat (g)
Dairy Products *(cont.)*						
Milk, fat-free or skim, 1 cup	83	12	0	8	Tr	Tr
Milk, whole, 3.25%, 1 cup	146	11	0	8	8	5
Milk shakes, chocolate, 10.6 oz	357	63	1	9	8	5
Yogurt, fruit, low-fat, 8 fl oz	243	46	0	10	3	2
Yogurt, plain, low-fat, 8 fl oz	154	17	0	13	4	2
Yogurt, vanilla, low-fat, 8 fl oz	208	34	0	12	3	2
FAST FOODS						
Biscuit, egg, cheese, and bacon, 1 biscuit	477	33	na	16	31	11
Cheeseburger, large, double patty, with condiments and vegetables, 1 sandwich	704	40	na	38	44	18
Cheeseburger, single patty, with condiments, 1 sandwich	295	27	na	16	14	6

Food, portion	Cal	Total Carb (g)	Fiber (g)	Protein (g)	Total Fat (g)	Sat Fat (g)
Chicken, breaded and fried, dark meat, 2 pieces	431	16	na	30	27	7
Chicken, breaded and fried, light meat, 2 pieces	494	20	na	36	30	8
Chicken fillet sandwich, plain, 1 sandwich	515	39	na	24	29	9
Chili con carne, 8 fl oz	256	22	na	25	8	3
Chimichanga, beef and cheese, 1 chimichanga	443	39	na	20	23	11
Coleslaw, ¾ cup	147	13	na	1	11	2
Crab cake, 1 cake	160	5	Tr	11	10	2
Croissant, egg and cheese, 1 croissant	368	24	na	13	25	14
Enchilada, cheese and beef, 1 enchilada	323	30	na	12	18	9
Fish fillet, battered or breaded, fried, 1 fillet	211	15	Tr	13	11	3

Food, portion	Cal	Total Carb (g)	Fiber (g)	Protein (g)	Total Fat (g)	Sat Fat (g)
Fast Foods (*CONT.*)						
Fish sandwich, with tartar sauce, 1 sandwich	431	41	na	17	23	5
French toast sticks, 5 pieces	513	58	3	8	29	5
Hamburger, double patty, with condiments, 1 sandwich	576	39	na	32	32	12
Hamburger, single patty, with condiments, 1 sandwich	272	34	2	12	10	4
Hot dog, plain, 1 sandwich	242	18	na	10	15	5
Ice milk, vanilla, soft-serve, with cone, 1 cone	164	24	Tr	4	6	4
Nachos, with cheese, 1 portion (6–8 nachos)	346	36	na	9	19	8
Onion rings, breaded and fried, 1 portion (8–9 onion rings)	276	31	na	4	16	7
Pizza with cheese, 1 slice	140	21	na	8	3	2

Food, portion	Cal	Total Carb (g)	Fiber (g)	Protein (g)	Total Fat (g)	Sat Fat (g)
Pizza with pepperoni, 1 slice	181	20	na	10	7	2
Potato, baked, with sour cream and chives, 1 serving	393	50	na	7	22	10
Potato, french fried in vegetable oil, 1 small order	291	34	3	4	16	3
Potato salad, ⅓ cup	108	13	na	1	6	1

Food, portion	Cal	Total Carb (g)	Fiber (g)	Protein (g)	Total Fat (g)	Sat Fat (g)
Fast Foods *(cont.)*						
Roast beef sandwich, plain, 1 sandwich	346	33	na	22	14	4
Salad, vegetable, tossed, without dressing, ¾ cup	17	3	na	1	Tr	Tr
Salad, vegetable, tossed, without dressing, with cheese and egg, 1½ cups	102	5	na	9	6	3
Shrimp, breaded and fried, 1 portion (6–8 shrimp)	454	40	na	19	25	5
Submarine sandwich, with cold cuts, 1 sandwich	456	51	na	22	19	7
Submarine sandwich, with tuna salad, 1 sandwich	584	55	na	30	28	5
Taco, 1 small	369	27	na	21	21	11
FATS AND OILS						
Butter, salted, 1 tbsp	102	Tr	0	Tr	12	6

Food, portion	Cal	Total Carb (g)	Fiber (g)	Protein (g)	Total Fat (g)	Sat Fat (g)
Lard, 1 tbsp	115	0	0	0	13	5
Margarine, stick, 80% fat, 1 tbsp	100	Tr	0	Tr	11	2
Margarine-butter blend, 60% corn oil margarine and 40% butter, 1 tsp	36	Tr	0	Tr	4	1
Margarine spread, fat-free, tub, 1 tbsp	6	1	0	Tr	Tr	Tr
Oil, olive, 1 tbsp	119	0	0	0	14	2
Oil, soybean, 1 tbsp	120	0	0	0	14	2
Oil, vegetable, canola, 1 tsp	40	0	0	0	5	Tr
Oil, vegetable, corn, 1 tsp	40	0	0	0	5	1
Salad dressing, French, 1 tbsp	73	2	0	Tr	7	1
Salad dressing, Italian, 1 tbsp	43	2	0	Tr	4	1
Salad dressing, ranch, 2 tbsp	148	1	Tr	Tr	16	2
Salad dressing, thousand island, 1 tbsp	59	2	Tr	Tr	6	1

Food, portion	Cal	Total Carb (g)	Fiber (g)	Protein (g)	Total Fat (g)	Sat Fat (g)
Fats and Oils *(cont.)*						
Salad dressing, vinegar and oil, 1 tbsp	72	Tr	0	0	8	1

FINFISH AND SHELLFISH PRODUCTS

Food, portion	Cal	Total Carb (g)	Fiber (g)	Protein (g)	Total Fat (g)	Sat Fat (g)
Catfish, cooked, 3 oz	89	0	0	16	2	1
Clam, raw, 1 medium	11	Tr	0	2	Tr	Tr
Cod, Atlantic, cooked, 3 oz	70	0	0	15	1	Tr
Crab, Alaska king, cooked, 1 leg	130	0	0	26	2	Tr
Crab, Dungeness, cooked, moist heat, 1 crab	140	1	0	28	2	Tr
Fish sticks, frozen, preheated, 1 stick (4"×1"×½")	76	7	Tr	4	3	1
Flatfish (flounder and sole), cooked, 1 fillet	149	0	0	31	2	Tr
Halibut, cooked, 3 oz	119	0	0	23	2	Tr

Food, portion	Cal	Total Carb (g)	Fiber (g)	Protein (g)	Total Fat (g)	Sat Fat (g)
Lobster, 1 lobster	135	1	0	28	1	Tr
Orange roughy, 3 oz	59	0	0	12	1	Tr
Salmon, pink, canned, solids with bone and liquid, 3 oz	118	0	0	17	5	1
Salmon, smoked (lox), 1 oz	33	0	0	5	1	Tr
Salmon, sockeye, cooked, 3 oz	184	0	0	23	9	2
Sardine, Atlantic, canned in oil, drained, with bones, 1 small	25	0	0	3	1	Tr
Scallops, breaded/fried, 2 large	67	3	0	6	3	1
Shrimp, 1 medium	6	Tr	0	1	Tr	Tr
Snapper, cooked, 3 oz	109	0	0	22	1	Tr
Surimi, 3 oz	84	6	0	13	1	Tr
Trout, rainbow, wild, cooked, 3 oz	128	0	0	19	5	1

Food, portion	Cal	Total Carb (g)	Fiber (g)	Protein (g)	Total Fat (g)	Sat Fat (g)
Finfish and Shellfish Products *(cont.)*						
Tuna, light, canned in water, drained, 1 can	191	0	0	42	1	Tr
Whitefish, smoked, 3 oz	92	0	0	20	1	Tr
FRUITS AND FRUIT JUICES						
Apple juice, unsweetened, 1 cup	117	29	Tr	Tr	Tr	Tr
Apples, raw, with skin, 1 medium (3 per lb)	72	19	3	Tr	Tr	Tr
Applesauce, sweetened, 1 cup	194	51	3	Tr	Tr	Tr
Apricots, juice pack, with skin, halves, 1 cup	117	30	4	2	Tr	Tr
Apricots, raw, 1 apricot	17	4	1	Tr	Tr	Tr
Avocados, raw, 1 cup, puréed	368	20	15	5	34	5
Bananas, raw, 1 medium	105	27	3	1	Tr	Tr

NUTRIENT COUNTER

Food, portion	Cal	Total Carb (g)	Fiber (g)	Protein (g)	Total Fat (g)	Sat Fat (g)
Blueberries, raw, 1 cup	83	21	3	1	Tr	Tr
Cantaloupe, raw, ⅛ melon	23	6	1	1	Tr	Tr
Casaba melon, raw, 1 melon	459	108	15	18	2	Tr
Cranberry sauce, canned, sweetened, 1 slice (½" thick)	86	22	1	Tr	Tr	Tr
Fruit cocktail, juice pack, 1 cup	109	28	2	1	Tr	Tr
Grapefruit, raw, ½ medium	41	10	1	1	Tr	Tr
Grapefruit juice, white, canned, sweetened, 1 cup	115	28	Tr	1	Tr	Tr
Grape juice, sweetened, 1 cup	128	32	Tr	Tr	Tr	Tr
Grapes, red or green, raw, seedless, 1 grape	3	1	Tr	Tr	Tr	Tr
Honeydew, ⅛ of 5¼" dia melon	45	11	1	1	Tr	Tr
Kiwi fruit, skinless, 1 medium	46	11	2	1	Tr	Tr

Food, portion	Cal	Total Carb (g)	Fiber (g)	Protein (g)	Total Fat (g)	Sat Fat (g)
Fruits and Fruit Juices *(cont.)*						
Mangoes, raw, 1 fruit	135	35	4	1	1	Tr
Nectarines, raw, 1 fruit	60	14	2	1	Tr	Tr
Orange juice, canned, unsweetened, 1 cup	105	25	Tr	1	Tr	Tr
Oranges, raw, 1 fruit	62	15	3	1	Tr	Tr
Peaches, canned, juice pack, halves or slices, 1 cup	109	29	3	2	Tr	Tr
Peaches, raw, 1 medium	38	9	1	1	Tr	Tr
Pears, canned, juice pack, 1 half, with liquid	38	10	1	Tr	Tr	Tr
Pears, raw, 1 medium pear	96	26	5	1	Tr	Tr
Pineapple, canned, juice pack, 1 cup, crushed, sliced, or chunks	149	39	2	1	Tr	Tr
Pineapple, raw, 1 slice	40	11	1	Tr	Tr	Tr

NUTRIENT COUNTER

Food, portion	Cal	Total Carb (g)	Fiber (g)	Protein (g)	Total Fat (g)	Sat Fat (g)
Plums, canned, purple, juice pack, 1 plum with liquid	27	7	Tr	Tr	Tr	Tr
Plums, raw, 1 fruit (2⅛"dia)	30	8	1	Tr	Tr	Tr
Prune juice, canned, 1 cup	182	45	3	2	Tr	Tr

FOOD, PORTION	CAL	TOTAL CARB (G)	FIBER (G)	PROTEIN (G)	TOTAL FAT (G)	SAT FAT (G)
FRUITS AND FRUIT JUICES (*CONT.*)						
Raisins, seedless, 1 box (.5 oz)	42	11	1	Tr	Tr	Tr
Strawberries, raw, 1 large	6	1	Tr	Tr	Tr	Tr
Tangerines, raw, 1 medium	37	9	2	1	Tr	Tr
Watermelon, raw, 1/16 of melon	86	22	1	2	Tr	Tr
LAMB AND VEAL						
Lamb, ground, broiled, 3 oz	241	0	0	21	17	7
Lamb, leg (shank and sirloin), roasted, 3 oz	219	0	0	22	14	6
Lamb, shoulder (arm and blade), roasted, 3 oz	235	0	0	19	17	7
Veal, boneless breast, braised, 3 oz	226	0	0	23	14	6
Veal, ground, broiled, 3 oz	146	0	0	21	6	3

Food, portion	Cal	Total Carb (g)	Fiber (g)	Protein (g)	Total Fat (g)	Sat Fat (g)
Veal, shoulder, roasted, 3 oz	156	0	0	22	7	3

LEGUMES AND LEGUME PRODUCTS

Food, portion	Cal	Total Carb (g)	Fiber (g)	Protein (g)	Total Fat (g)	Sat Fat (g)
Bacon, meatless, 1 strip	16	Tr	Tr	1	1	Tr
Beans, baked, canned, plain or vegetarian, 1 cup	236	52	13	12	1	Tr
Beans, black, boiled, 1 cup	227	41	15	15	1	Tr
Beans, Great Northern, boiled, 1 cup	209	37	12	15	1	Tr
Beans, kidney, boiled, 1 cup	225	40	11	15	1	Tr
Chickpeas (garbanzo beans), boiled, 1 cup	269	45	12	15	4	Tr
Chili with beans, canned, 1 cup	287	30	11	15	14	6
Cowpeas (blackeye, crowder, Southern), boiled, 1 cup	198	35	11	13	1	Tr
Hummus, 1 tbsp	27	3	1	1	1	Tr

NUTRIENT COUNTER

Food, portion	Cal	Total Carb (g)	Fiber (g)	Protein (g)	Total Fat (g)	Sat Fat (g)
LEGUMES AND LEGUME PRODUCTS *(CONT.)*						
Lentils, boiled, 1 cup	230	40	16	18	1	Tr
Peanut butter, smooth, 2 tbsp	192	6	2	8	17	3
Peanuts, dry-roasted, without salt, 1 cup	854	31	12	35	73	10
Sausage, meatless, 1 link	64	2	1	5	5	1
Soy milk, fluid, 1 cup	120	11	3	9	5	1
Soy sauce (tamari), 1 tbsp	11	1	Tr	2	Tr	Tr
Tempeh, 1 cup	320	16	na	31	18	4
Tofu, firm, prepared with calcium sulfate and magnesium chloride (nigari), ¼ block	62	2	Tr	7	4	1
NUT AND SEED PRODUCTS						
Almonds, 1 cup, whole	827	28	17	30	72	6

Food, portion	Cal	Total Carb (g)	Fiber (g)	Protein (g)	Total Fat (g)	Sat Fat (g)
Cashew nuts, dry-roasted, with salt added, 1 cup	786	45	4	21	63	13
Mixed nuts, oil-roasted, with peanuts, with salt added, 1 cup	876	30	13	24	80	12
Pecans, 1 oz (20 halves)	196	4	3	3	20	2
Pistachio nuts, dry-roasted, without salt added, 1 cup	702	34	13	26	57	7
Sunflower seed kernels, dried, without hulls, 1 cup	821	27	15	33	71	7
Walnuts, English, 7 nuts	183	4	2	4	18	2

PORK PRODUCTS

Food, portion	Cal	Total Carb (g)	Fiber (g)	Protein (g)	Total Fat (g)	Sat Fat (g)
Backribs, fresh, roasted, 1 piece	810	0	0	53	65	24
Bacon, cured, pan-fried, 1 slice	42	Tr	0	3	3	1
Canadian-style bacon, cured, grilled, 2 slices (6 per 6-oz pkg)	87	1	0	11	4	1

FOOD, PORTION	CAL	TOTAL CARB (G)	FIBER (G)	PROTEIN (G)	TOTAL FAT (G)	SAT FAT (G)
PORK PRODUCTS (*CONT.*)						
Ground pork, cooked, 3 oz	252	0	0	22	18	7
Ham, cured, boneless, extra-lean (approx 5% fat), roasted, 3 oz	123	1	0	18	5	2
Ham, cured, regular (approx 13% fat), canned, roasted, 3 oz	192	Tr	0	17	13	4
Loin, blade (chops), fresh, bone-in, pan-fried, 1 chop	284	0	0	18	23	8
Loin, fresh, sirloin (roasts), boneless, roasted, 3 oz	176	0	0	24	8	3
POULTRY PRODUCTS						
Chicken, breast, meat and skin, batter-fried, ½ breast	364	13	Tr	35	18	5
Chicken, breast, meat and skin, roasted, ½ breast	193	0	0	29	8	2
Chicken, canned, no broth, 5 oz can	230	1	0	32	10	3

NUTRIENT COUNTER

Food, portion	Cal	Total Carb (g)	Fiber (g)	Protein (g)	Total Fat (g)	Sat Fat (g)
Chicken, drumstick, meat and skin, batter-fried, 1 drumstick	193	6	Tr	16	11	3
Chicken, drumstick, meat and skin, roasted, 1 drumstick	112	0	0	14	6	2
Chicken, roasting, light meat only, roasted, 1 cup chopped	214	0	0	38	6	2
Chicken, wing, meat and skin, batter-fried, 1 wing	159	5	Tr	10	11	3
Chicken, wing, meat and skin, roasted, 1 wing	99	0	0	9	7	2
Cornish game hens, meat and skin, roasted, 1 whole bird	668	0	0	57	47	13
Duck, roasted, ½ duck	1287	0	0	73	108	37
Turkey, ground, cooked, 1 patty (4 oz raw)	193	0	0	22	11	3
Turkey, leg, meat and skin, roasted, 1 leg	1136	0	0	152	54	17

Food, portion	Cal	Total Carb (g)	Fiber (g)	Protein (g)	Total Fat (g)	Sat Fat (g)
SAUSAGE AND LUNCHEON MEATS						
Beef, cured, sausage, cooked, smoked, 1 sausage	134	1	0	6	12	5
Beef, thin sliced, 5 slices	37	1	0	6	1	Tr
Bologna, beef, 1 slice	87	1	0	3	8	3
Bologna, turkey, 1 slice	59	1	Tr	3	4	1
Frankfurter, beef, 1 frankfurter	149	2	0	5	13	5
Ham, sliced, regular, 1 slice	46	1	Tr	5	2	1
Pastrami, cured, 1 slice (1 oz)	98	1	0	5	8	3
Pepperoni, pork/beef, 15 slices	135	1	Tr	6	12	5
Salami, cooked, beef, 1 slice	67	Tr	0	3	6	3
Salami, dry or hard, pork, 1 slice (3⅛" dia×1/16" thick)	41	Tr	0	2	3	1

Food, portion	Cal	Total Carb (g)	Fiber (g)	Protein (g)	Total Fat (g)	Sat Fat (g)
Sausage, Italian, pork, cooked, 1 link (4 links per lb)	268	1	0	17	21	8
Sausage, pork, cooked, 1 link	81	0	0	5	7	2
Turkey breast meat, 1 slice	27	4	1	2	Tr	Tr

SNACKS

Food, portion	Cal	Total Carb (g)	Fiber (g)	Protein (g)	Total Fat (g)	Sat Fat (g)
Beef jerky, 1 piece, large	82	2	Tr	7	5	2
BETTY CROCKER Fruit Roll Ups, berry-flavored, 2 rolls	104	24	na	Tr	1	Tr
Corn chips, plain, 1 bag (7 oz)	1067	113	10	13	66	9
Granola bar, soft, uncoated, nut and raisin, 1 bar (1 oz)	127	18	2	2	6	3
Popcorn, air-popped, 1 cup	31	6	1	1	Tr	Tr
Pork skins, plain, ½ oz	77	0	0	9	4	2
Potato chips, plain, salted, 8 oz	1217	120	10	16	79	25

NUTRIENT COUNTER

FOOD, PORTION	CAL	TOTAL CARB (G)	FIBER (G)	PROTEIN (G)	TOTAL FAT (G)	SAT FAT (G)
SNACKS (CONT.)						
Pretzels, hard, salted, 10 twists	229	48	2	5	2	Tr
Tortilla chips, plain, 1 oz	142	18	2	2	7	1
Trail mix, 1 cup	693	67	na	21	44	8
SOUPS, SAUCES, AND GRAVIES						
Gravy, beef or brown, 1 serving	25	4	Tr	1	1	Tr

Food, portion	Cal	Total Carb (g)	Fiber (g)	Protein (g)	Total Fat (g)	Sat Fat (g)
Sauce, barbecue, 8 fl oz	188	32	3	5	5	1
Sauce, cheese, ¼ cup	110	4	Tr	4	8	4
Sauce, pasta, spaghetti/marinara, 1 cup	143	21	4	4	5	1
Sauce, salsa, ½ cup	36	8	2	2	Tr	Tr
Soup, beef broth, 8 fl oz	29	2	0	5	0	0
Soup, chicken noodle, canned, prepared with equal volume water, 8 fl oz	75	9	1	4	2	1
Soup, clam chowder, New England, canned, prepared with equal volume milk, 1 cup	164	17	1	9	7	3
Soup, cream of mushroom, canned, prepared with equal volume milk, 8 fl oz	203	15	Tr	6	14	5
Soup, minestrone, canned, prepared with equal volume water, 8 fl oz	82	11	1	4	3	1
Soup, split pea with ham, chunky, ready-to-serve, 1 cup	185	27	4	11	4	2

Food, portion	Cal	Total Carb (g)	Fiber (g)	Protein (g)	Total Fat (g)	Sat Fat (g)
SOUPS, SAUCES, AND GRAVIES *(CONT.)*						
Soup, tomato, canned, prepared with equal volume water, 8 fl oz	85	17	Tr	2	2	Tr
Soup, vegetable beef, canned, prepared with equal volume water, 8 fl oz	78	10	Tr	6	2	1
SWEETS						
Frosting (chocolate, creamy, ready-to-eat), 2 tbsp	163	26	Tr	Tr	7	2
Frozen juice novelties, fruit and juice bars, 1 bar (2.5 fl oz)	63	16	1	1	Tr	0
Frozen yogurts, chocolate, soft-serve, ½ cup (4 fl oz)	115	18	2	3	4	3
Gelatin desserts, dry mix, prepared with water, ½ cup	84	19	0	2	0	0
Gumdrops, 10 gummy bears	87	22	Tr	0	0	0
Honey, 1 tbsp	64	17	Tr	Tr	0	0

Food, portion	Cal	Total Carb (g)	Fiber (g)	Protein (g)	Total Fat (g)	Sat Fat (g)
Ice cream, chocolate, ½ cup	143	19	1	3	7	4
Jams and preserves, 1 tbsp	56	14	Tr	Tr	Tr	Tr
"M&M's" Milk Chocolate Candies, 10 pieces	34	5	Tr	Tr	1	1
Marshmallows, 1 regular	23	6	Tr	Tr	Tr	Tr
Milk chocolate, 1 bar (1.55 oz)	235	26	1	3	13	6
MILKY WAY Bar, 1 bar (.8 oz)	97	16	Tr	1	4	2
Puddings, chocolate, ready-to-eat, 1 can (5 oz)	197	33	1	4	6	1
Semisweet chocolate chips, 1 cup (6 oz package)	805	106	10	7	50	30
Sherbet, orange, ½ cup (4 fl oz)	107	22	2	1	1	1
SKITTLES, 10 pieces	43	10	0	Tr	Tr	Tr
Sugars, brown, 1 cup, packed	829	214	0	0	0	0

Food, portion	Cal	Total Carb (g)	Fiber (g)	Protein (g)	Total Fat (g)	Sat Fat (g)
Sweets *(cont.)*						
Sugar, granulated, 1 tsp	16	4	0	0	0	0
Sugar, granulated, 1 cup	774	200	0	0	0	0
Syrup, chocolate, fudge, 2 tbsp	133	24	1	2	3	2
Syrup, pancake, 1 tbsp	47	12	Tr	0	0	0
VEGETABLES AND VEGETABLE PRODUCTS						
Asparagus, boiled, 4 spears	13	2	1	1	Tr	Tr
Beans, snap, green, boiled, 1 cup	44	10	4	2	Tr	Tr
Broccoli, raw, 1 cup chopped	30	6	2	2	Tr	Tr
Cabbage, raw, shredded, 1 cup	17	4	2	1	Tr	Tr
Carrots, raw, 1 medium	25	6	2	1	Tr	Tr
Cauliflower, boiled, ½ cup	14	3	2	1	Tr	Tr
Cauliflower, raw, 1 floweret	3	1	Tr	Tr	Tr	Tr

Food, portion	Cal	Total Carb (g)	Fiber (g)	Protein (g)	Total Fat (g)	Sat Fat (g)
Celery, raw, 1 medium stalk	6	1	1	Tr	Tr	Tr
Coleslaw, ½ cup	41	7	1	1	2	Tr
Corn, sweet, boiled, 1 ear	83	19	2	3	1	Tr
Corn, sweet, canned, whole kernel, 1 cup	133	30	3	4	2	Tr
Cucumber, ½ cup slices	8	2	Tr	Tr	Tr	Tr
Eggplant, boiled, 1 cup cubes	35	9	2	1	Tr	Tr
Mushrooms, raw, 1 medium	4	1	Tr	1	Tr	Tr
Onions, raw, 1 slice (⅛" thick)	6	1	Tr	Tr	Tr	Tr
Peas, green, boiled, 1 cup	134	25	9	9	Tr	Tr
Peppers, sweet, green, raw, 1 medium	24	6	2	1	Tr	Tr
Pickle, dill, 1 medium	12	3	1	Tr	Tr	Tr
Potatoes, baked, flesh, 1 potato	145	34	2	3	Tr	Tr

NUTRIENT COUNTER

Food, portion	Cal	Total Carb (g)	Fiber (g)	Protein (g)	Total Fat (g)	Sat Fat (g)
VEGETABLES AND VEGETABLE PRODUCTS (CONT.)						
Potatoes, french fried, frozen, oven-heated, 10 strips	100	16	2	2	4	1
Potatoes, hashed brown, 1 cup	413	55	5	5	20	2
Potatoes, mashed, whole milk added, 1 cup	174	37	3	4	1	1
Potato salad, 1 cup	358	28	3	7	21	4
Pumpkin, canned, 1 cup	83	20	7	3	1	Tr
Spinach, frozen, chopped or leaf, boiled, ½ cup	30	5	4	4	Tr	Tr
Squash, summer, all varieties, raw, sliced, 1 cup	18	4	1	1	Tr	Tr
Squash, winter, acorn, baked, cubes, 1 cup	115	30	9	2	Tr	Tr
Sweet potato, baked in skin, 1 medium	103	24	4	2	Tr	Tr

Food, portion	Cal	Total Carb (g)	Fiber (g)	Protein (g)	Total Fat (g)	Sat Fat (g)
Tomato, raw, 1 medium	22	5	1	1	Tr	Tr
Tomatoes, stewed, 1 cup	66	16	3	2	Tr	Tr
Tomatoes, sun-dried, packed in oil, drained, 1 cup	234	26	6	6	15	2
Tomato juice, canned, with salt added, 1 cup	41	10	1	2	Tr	Tr
Tomato paste, canned, 1 cup	215	50	12	11	1	Tr
Tomato sauce, with mushrooms, canned, 1 cup	86	21	4	4	Tr	Tr
Vegetables, mixed, frozen, boiled, ½ cup	59	12	4	3	Tr	Tr

HAM & CHEDDAR FRITTATA

MAKES 4 SERVINGS ✦ NET CARB COUNT: 4 GRAMS

- 3 **eggs**
- 3 **egg whites**
- ½ **teaspoon salt**
- ½ **teaspoon freshly ground black pepper**
- 1½ **cups (4 ounces) frozen broccoli florets, thawed**
- 6 **ounces deli smoked ham, cut into ½-inch cubes (1¼ cups)**
- ⅓ **cup drained bottled roasted red bell peppers, cut into thin strips**
- 1 **tablespoon butter**
- ½ **cup (2 ounces) shredded sharp Cheddar cheese**

1. Preheat broiler.

2. Beat eggs, egg whites, salt and black pepper in large bowl until blended. Stir in broccoli, ham and bell pepper strips.

3. Melt butter over medium heat in 10-inch ovenproof skillet with sloping side. Pour egg mixture into skillet; cover. Cook 5 to 6 minutes or until eggs are set around edge. (Center will be wet.)

4. Uncover; sprinkle cheese over frittata. Transfer skillet to broiler; broil, 5 inches from heat source, 2 minutes or until eggs are set in center and cheese is melted. Let stand 5 minutes; cut into wedges.

Nutrients per Serving: Calories 210; Total Fat 13g; Saturated Fat 6g; Protein 19g; Total Carbohydrates 5g; Fiber 1g; Cholesterol 201mg; Sodium 995mg

CRUSTLESS INDIVIDUAL SPINACH & BACON QUICHE

MAKES 10 SERVINGS ✦ NET CARB COUNT: 3 GRAMS

3 **strips bacon**

½ **small onion, diced**

1 **package (9 ounces) frozen chopped spinach, thawed, drained and squeezed dry**

½ **teaspoon black pepper**

⅛ **teaspoon ground nutmeg**

  Pinch salt

1 **container (15-ounces) whole milk ricotta cheese**

2 **cups (8 ounces) shredded mozzarella cheese**

1 **cup (4 ounces) grated Parmesan cheese**

3 **eggs, beaten slightly**

1. Preheat oven to 350°F. Spray muffin pan with nonstick cooking spray.

2. Cook bacon in large skillet on medium-high heat until crisp. Drain, cool and crumble.

3. In same skillet, cook and stir onion in remaining bacon fat 5 minutes or until tender. Add spinach, pepper, nutmeg and salt. Cook and stir over medium heat about 3 minutes or until liquid evaporates. Return bacon to skillet and remove from heat.

4. Combine ricotta, mozzarella and Parmesan cheeses in large bowl; mix in eggs. Add cooled spinach mixture and combine well.

5. Divide mixture evenly to fill 10 muffin cups. Bake 40 minutes or until filling is set. Let stand 10 minutes. Run thin knife around edges to release. Serve hot or refrigerate and serve cold.

Nutrients per Serving: Calories 216; Total Fat 15g; Saturated Fat 9g; Protein 17g; Total Carbohydrates 4g; Fiber 1g; Cholesterol 105mg; Sodium 405mg

FETA BRUNCH BAKE

MAKES 4 SERVINGS ✦ NET CARB COUNT: 6 GRAMS

1 **medium red bell pepper**

2 **bags (10 ounces each) fresh spinach, washed and stemmed**

6 **eggs**

6 **ounces crumbled feta cheese**

⅓ **cup chopped onion**

2 **tablespoons chopped fresh parsley**

¼ **teaspoon dried dill weed**

Dash black pepper

1. Preheat broiler. Place bell pepper on foil-lined broiler pan. Broil, 4 inches from heat, 15 to 20 minutes or until blackened on all sides, turning every 5 minutes with tongs. Place in paper bag; close bag and set aside to cool about 15 to 20 minutes. To peel pepper, cut around core, twist and remove. Cut in half and peel off skin with paring knife; rinse under cold water to remove seeds. Cut into ½-inch pieces.

2. To blanch spinach, heat 1 quart water in 2-quart saucepan over high heat to a boil. Add spinach. Return to a boil; boil 2 to 3 minutes until crisp-tender. Drain and immediately plunge into cold water. Drain; let stand until cool enough to handle. Squeeze spinach to remove excess water; finely chop.

3. Preheat oven to 400°F. Grease 1-quart baking dish. Beat eggs in large bowl with electric mixer at medium speed until foamy. Stir in bell pepper, spinach, cheese, onion, parsley, dill and pepper. Pour egg mixture into prepared dish. Bake 20 minutes or until set. Let stand 5 minutes before serving. Garnish as desired.

Nutrients per Serving: Calories 266; Total Fat 17g; Saturated Fat 9g; Protein 20g; Total Carbohydrates 10g; Fiber 4g; Cholesterol 359mg; Sodium 684mg

BRUNCH EGGS OLÉ

MAKES 8 SERVINGS ✦ NET CARB COUNT: 10 GRAMS

8	**eggs**
½	**cup all-purpose flour**
1	**teaspoon baking powder**
¾	**teaspoon salt**
2	**cups (8 ounces) shredded Monterey Jack cheese with jalapeño peppers**
1½	**cups (12 ounces) small curd cottage cheese**
1	**cup (4 ounces) shredded sharp Cheddar cheese**
1	**jalapeño pepper,* seeded and chopped**
½	**teaspoon hot pepper sauce**
	Fresh Salsa (recipe follows)

*Jalapeño peppers can sting and irritate the skin; wear rubber gloves when handling peppers and do not touch eyes. Wash hands after handling.

1. Preheat oven to 350°F. Grease 9-inch square baking pan.

2. Beat eggs in large bowl at high speed of electric mixer 4 to 5 minutes or until slightly thickened and lemon-colored.

3. Combine flour, baking powder and salt in small bowl. Stir flour mixture into eggs until blended.

4. Combine Monterey Jack cheese, cottage cheese, Cheddar cheese, jalapeño and hot pepper sauce in medium bowl; mix well. Fold into egg mixture until well blended. Pour into prepared pan.

5. Bake 45 to 50 minutes or until golden brown and firm in center. Let stand 10 minutes before cutting into 8 slices to serve. Serve with Fresh Salsa. Garnish as desired.

Nutrients per Serving: Calories 321; Total Fat 20g; Saturated Fat 10g; Protein 24g; Total Carbohydrates 11g; Fiber 1g; Cholesterol 261mg; Sodium 871mg

Fresh Salsa

   3 medium plum tomatoes, seeded and chopped
   2 tablespoons chopped onion
   1 small jalapeño pepper,* stemmed, seeded and minced
   1 tablespoon chopped fresh cilantro
   1 tablespoon lime juice
 ¼ teaspoon salt
 ⅛ teaspoon black pepper

*Jalapeño peppers can sting and irritate the skin; wear rubber gloves when handling peppers and do not touch eyes. Wash hands after handling.

Combine tomatoes, onion, jalapeño pepper, cilantro, lime juice, salt and black pepper in small bowl. Refrigerate until ready to serve.

Makes 1 cup

APPLE AND BRIE OMELET

MAKES 4 SERVINGS ✦ NET CARB COUNT: 10 GRAMS

2 **large Golden Delicious apples**

2 **tablespoons butter or margarine, divided**

½ **teaspoon ground nutmeg**

4 **ounces Brie cheese**

8 **large eggs, lightly beaten**

2 **green onions, thinly sliced**

1. Place large serving platter in oven and preheat to 200°F. Peel, core and slice apples; place in microwavable container. Top with 1 tablespoon butter and nutmeg. Cover and microwave at HIGH (100% power) 3 minutes. Set aside. While apples cook, trim rind from cheese; thinly slice cheese.

2. Melt 1½ teaspoons butter in medium nonstick skillet over medium heat; rotate skillet to coat bottom. Place eggs in medium bowl and whisk until blended. Pour half of eggs into skillet. Let cook, without stirring, 1 to 2 minutes, or until set on bottom. With rubber spatula, lift side of omelet and slightly tilt pan to allow uncooked portion of egg to flow underneath. Cover pan and cook 2 to 3 minutes, until eggs are set but still moist on top. Remove platter from oven and slide omelet into center. Spread apples evenly over entire omelet, reserving a few slices for garnish, if desired. Evenly space cheese slices over apples. Sprinkle with onion, reserving some for garnish. Return platter to oven.

3. Cook remaining beaten eggs in remaining 1½ teaspoons butter as directed above. When cooked, slide spatula around edge to be certain omelet is loose. Carefully place second omelet over cheese, apple and onion mixture. Top with reserved apple and onion slices. Cut into wedges to serve.

Nutrients per Serving: Calories 334; Total Fat 24g; Saturated Fat 11g; Protein 19g; Total Carbohydrates 11g; Fiber 1g; Cholesterol 469mg; Sodium 362mg

EASY BRUNCH FRITTATA

MAKES 6 SERVINGS ✦ NET CARB COUNT: 10 GRAMS

Nonstick cooking spray

1 **cup small broccoli florets**

2½ **cups (12 ounces) frozen hash brown potatoes with onions and peppers (O'Brien style), thawed**

1½ **cups cholesterol-free egg substitute, thawed**

2 **tablespoons reduced-fat (2%) milk**

¾ **teaspoon salt**

¼ **teaspoon black pepper**

½ **cup (2 ounces) shredded reduced-fat Cheddar cheese**

Sour cream (optional)

1. Preheat oven to 450°F. Coat medium nonstick ovenproof skillet with cooking spray. Heat skillet over medium heat until hot. Add broccoli; cook and stir 2 minutes. Add potatoes; cook and stir 5 minutes.

2. Beat together egg substitute, milk, salt and pepper in small bowl; pour over potato mixture. Cook 5 minutes or until edge is set (center will still be wet).

3. Transfer skillet to oven; bake 6 minutes or until center is set. Remove from oven. Sprinkle with cheese; let stand 2 to 3 minutes or until cheese is melted.

4. Cut into wedges; serve with sour cream, if desired.

Nutrients per Serving: Calories 102; Total Fat 2g; Saturated Fat 1g; Protein 9g; Total Carbohydrates 11g; Fiber 1g; Cholesterol 7mg; Sodium 627mg

GREEK ISLES OMELET

MAKES 2 SERVINGS ✦ NET CARB COUNT: 6 GRAMS

Nonstick cooking spray
¼ **cup chopped onion**
¼ **cup canned artichoke hearts, rinsed and drained**
¼ **cup washed and torn spinach leaves**
¼ **cup chopped plum tomato**
 I **cup cholesterol-free egg substitute**
 2 **tablespoons sliced pitted ripe olives, rinsed and drained**
Dash black pepper

1. Spray small nonstick skillet with cooking spray; heat over medium heat until hot. Cook and stir onion 2 minutes or until crisp-tender.

2. Add artichoke hearts. Cook and stir until heated through. Add spinach and tomato; toss briefly. Remove from heat. Transfer vegetables to small bowl. Wipe out skillet and spray with cooking spray.

3. Combine egg substitute, olives and pepper in medium bowl. Heat skillet over medium heat until hot. Pour egg mixture into skillet. Cook over medium heat 5 to 7 minutes; as eggs begin to set, gently lift edge of omelet with spatula and tilt skillet so uncooked portion flows underneath.

4. When egg mixture is set, spoon vegetable mixture over half of omelet. Loosen omelet with spatula and fold in half. Slide omelet onto serving plate.

Nutrients per Serving: Calories 111; Total Fat 3g; Saturated Fat <1g; Protein 13g; Total Carbohydrates 7g; Fiber 1g; Cholesterol 0; Sodium 538mg

MEXICAN OMELET ROLL-UPS WITH AVOCADO SAUCE

MAKES 8 SERVINGS ✦ NET CARB COUNT: 14 GRAMS

8	**eggs**
2	**tablespoons milk**
1	**tablespoon margarine or butter**
1½	**cups (6 ounces) shredded Monterey Jack cheese**
1	**large tomato, seeded and chopped**
¼	**cup chopped fresh cilantro**
8	**(7-inch) corn tortillas**
1½	**cups salsa**
2	**medium avocados, chopped**
¼	**cup reduced-fat sour cream**
2	**tablespoons diced green chilies**
1	**tablespoon fresh lemon juice**
1	**teaspoon hot pepper sauce**
¼	**teaspoon salt**

1. Preheat oven to 350°F. Spray 13×9-inch baking dish with nonstick cooking spray.

2. Whisk eggs and milk in medium bowl until blended. Melt margarine in large skillet over medium heat; add egg mixture to skillet. Cook and stir 5 minutes or until eggs are set, but still soft. Remove from heat. Stir in cheese, tomato and cilantro.

3. Spoon about ⅓ cup egg mixture evenly down center of each tortilla. Roll up tortillas and place seam side down in prepared dish. Pour salsa evenly over tortillas. Cover tightly with foil and bake 20 minutes or until heated through.

4. Meanwhile, process avocados, sour cream, chilies, lemon juice, hot pepper sauce and salt in food processor or blender until smooth. Serve tortillas with avocado sauce.

Cook's Nook: To reduce amount of fat in recipe, omit avocado sauce and serve with additional salsa and nonfat sour cream.

Nutrients per Serving: Calories 320; Total Fat 21g; Saturated Fat 7g; Protein 15g; Total Carbohydrates 19g; Fiber 5g; Cholesterol 237mg; Sodium 476mg

BREAKFAST

SPICY CRABMEAT FRITTATA

MAKES 4 SERVINGS ✦ NET CARB COUNT: 4 GRAMS

- 1 tablespoon olive oil
- 1 medium green bell pepper, finely chopped
- 2 cloves garlic, minced
- 6 eggs
- 1 can (6½ ounces) lump white crabmeat, drained
- ¼ teaspoon black pepper
- ¼ teaspoon salt
- ¼ teaspoon pepper sauce
- 1 large ripe plum tomato, seeded and finely chopped

1. Preheat broiler. Heat oil in 10-inch nonstick skillet with ovenproof handle over medium-high heat. Add bell pepper and garlic; cook and stir 3 minutes or until soft.

2. Meanwhile, beat eggs in medium bowl. Break up large pieces of crabmeat. Add crabmeat, black pepper, salt and pepper sauce to eggs; blend well. Set aside.

3. Add tomato to skillet; cook and stir 1 minute. Add egg mixture. Reduce heat to medium-low; cook about 7 minutes or until eggs begin to set around edges.

4. Remove pan from burner and place under broiler 6 inches from heat. Broil about 2 minutes or until frittata is set and top is browned. Remove from broiler; slide frittata onto serving plate. Serve immediately.

Nutrients per Serving: Calories 187; Total Fat 11g; Saturated Fat 3g; Protein 17g; Total Carbohydrates 4g; Fiber <1g; Cholesterol 358mg; Sodium 580mg

JERK WINGS WITH RANCH DIPPING SAUCE

MAKES 10 SERVINGS ✦ NET CARB COUNT: 2 GRAMS

½ **cup mayonnaise**

½ **cup plain yogurt or sour cream**

1½ **teaspoons salt, divided**

1¼ **teaspoons garlic powder, divided**

½ **teaspoon black pepper, divided**

¼ **teaspoon onion powder**

2 **tablespoons orange juice**

1 **teaspoon sugar**

1 **teaspoon dried thyme leaves**

1 **teaspoon paprika**

¼ **teaspoon ground nutmeg**

¼ **teaspoon ground red pepper**

2½ **pounds chicken wings (about 10 wings)**

1. Preheat oven to 450°F. Spray broiler pan with nonstick cooking spray. For Ranch Dipping Sauce, combine mayonnaise, yogurt, ½ teaspoon salt, ¼ teaspoon garlic powder, ¼ teaspoon black pepper and onion powder in small bowl.

2. Combine orange juice, sugar, thyme, paprika, nutmeg, red pepper, remaining 1 teaspoon salt, 1 teaspoon garlic powder and ¼ teaspoon black pepper in small bowl.

3. Cut tips from wings; discard. Place wings in large bowl. Drizzle with orange juice mixture; toss to coat.

4. Transfer chicken to greased broiler pan. Bake 25 to 30 minutes or until juices run clear and skin is crisp. Serve with Ranch Dipping Sauce.

Serving Suggestion: Serve with celery sticks.

Nutrients per Serving (1 wing plus about 2 tablespoons sauce): Calories 200; Total Fat 17g; Saturated Fat 4g; Protein 10g; Total Carbohydrates 2g; Fiber <1g; Cholesterol 69mg; Sodium 427mg

SMOKED SALMON ROSES

MAKES 32 SERVINGS ✦ NET CARB COUNT: 1 GRAM

1	**package (8 ounces) cream cheese, softened**
1	**tablespoon prepared horseradish**
1	**tablespoon minced fresh dill plus whole sprigs for garnish**
1	**tablespoon half-and-half**
16	**slices (12 to 16 ounces) smoked salmon**
1	**red bell pepper, cut into thin strips**

1. Combine cream cheese, horseradish, minced dill and half-and-half in a bowl. Beat until light.

2. Spread 1 tablespoon cream cheese mixture over each salmon slice. Roll up jelly-roll fashion from the long end. Slice each roll in half widthwise. Stand salmon rolls, cut side up, on a serving dish to resemble roses. Garnish each "rose" by tucking 1 pepper strip and 1 dill sprig in center.

Nutrients per Serving (1 "rose"): Calories 40; Total Fat 3g; Saturated Fat 2g; Protein 3g; Total Carbohydrates 1g; Fiber <1g; Cholesterol 10mg; Sodium 106mg

HAM AND CHEESE "SUSHI" ROLLS

MAKES 8 SERVINGS ✦ NET CARB COUNT: 3 GRAMS

4 **thin slices deli ham (about 4×4 inches)**
1 **package (8 ounces) cream cheese, softened**
1 **seedless cucumber, quartered lengthwise and cut into 4-inch lengths**
4 **thin slices (about 4×4 inches) American or Cheddar cheese, room temperature**
1 **red bell pepper, cut into thin 4-inch-long strips**

1. For ham sushi: Pat 1 ham slice with paper towel to remove excess moisture. Spread 2 tablespoons cream cheese to edges of ham slice. Pat 1 cucumber quarter with paper towel to remove excess moisture; place at edge of ham slice. Roll tightly, pressing gently to seal. Wrap in plastic wrap; refrigerate. Repeat with remaining 3 ham slices.

2. For cheese sushi: Spread 2 tablespoons cream cheese to edges of 1 cheese slice. Place 2 strips red pepper even with one edge of one cheese slice. Roll tightly. Seal by pressing gently. Wrap in plastic wrap; refrigerate. Repeat with remaining 3 cheese slices.

3. To serve: Remove plastic wrap from ham and cheese rolls. Cut each roll into 8 (½-inch-wide) pieces. Arrange on plate.

Nutrients per Serving (8 pieces): Calories 145; Total Fat 13g; Saturated Fat 12g; Protein 5g; Total Carbohydrates 3g; Fiber <1g; Cholesterol 40mg; Sodium 263mg

CRAB CANAPÉS

MAKES 16 SERVINGS ✦ NET CARB COUNT: 4 GRAMS

⅔ **cup fat-free cream cheese, softened**

2 **teaspoons lemon juice**

1 **teaspoon hot pepper sauce**

1 **package (8 ounces) imitation crabmeat or lobster, flaked**

⅓ **cup chopped red bell pepper**

2 **green onions with tops, sliced (about ¼ cup)**

64 **cucumber slices (about 2½ medium cucumbers cut into ⅜-inch-thick slices)**

Fresh parsley, for garnish (optional)

1. Combine cream cheese, lemon juice and hot pepper sauce in medium bowl; mix well. Stir in crabmeat, bell pepper and green onions; cover. Chill until ready to serve.

2. When ready to serve, spoon 1½ teaspoons crabmeat mixture onto each cucumber slice. Place on serving plate; garnish with parsley, if desired.

Tip: To allow flavors to blend, chill crab mixture at least 1 hour before spreading onto cucumbers or melba toast rounds.

Nutrients per Serving: (4 canapés): Calories 31 (8% of calories from fat); Total Fat <1g; Saturated Fat <1g; Protein 4g; Total Carbohydrates 4g; Fiber <1g; Cholesterol 5mg; Sodium 178mg

HERBED STUFFED TOMATOES

MAKES 5 SERVINGS ✦ NET CARB COUNT: 3 GRAMS

15 **cherry tomatoes**

½ **cup low-fat (1%) cottage cheese**

1 **tablespoon thinly sliced green onion**

1 **teaspoon chopped fresh chervil or ¼ teaspoon dried chervil leaves**

½ **teaspoon snipped fresh dill or ⅛ teaspoon dried dill weed**

⅛ **teaspoon lemon pepper**

1. Cut thin slice off bottom of each tomato. Scoop out pulp with small spoon; discard pulp. Invert tomatoes onto paper towels to drain.

2. Combine cottage cheese, green onion, chervil, dill and lemon pepper in small bowl. Spoon into tomatoes. Serve at once, or cover and refrigerate up to 8 hours.

Nutrients per Serving (3 stuffed tomatoes): Calories 27; Total Fat <1g; Saturated Fat <1g; Protein 3g; Total Carbohydrates 3g; Fiber <1g; Cholesterol 1mg; Sodium 96mg

JICAMA & SHRIMP COCKTAIL WITH ROASTED RED PEPPER SAUCE

MAKES 8 SERVINGS ✦ NET CARB COUNT: 9 GRAMS

- 2 **large red bell peppers**
- 6 **ounces (about 24 medium-large) shrimp, peeled and deveined**
- 1 **medium clove garlic**
- 1½ **cups fresh cilantro sprigs**
- 2 **tablespoons lime juice**
- 2 **tablespoons orange juice**
- ½ **teaspoon hot pepper sauce**
- 1 **small jicama (about ¾ pound), peeled and cut into strips**
- 1 **plum tomato, halved, seeded and thinly sliced**

1. Preheat broiler. Place bell peppers on broiler pan. Broil, 4 to 6 inches from heat, about 6 minutes, turning every 2 to 3 minutes or until all sides are charred. Transfer peppers to paper bag; close bag tightly. Let stand 10 minutes or until peppers are cool enough to handle and skins are loosened. Peel peppers; cut in half. Remove cores, seeds and membranes; discard.

2. Add shrimp to large saucepan of boiling water. Reduce heat to medium-low; simmer, uncovered, 2 to 3 minutes or until shrimp turn pink. Drain shrimp; rinse under cold running water. Cover; refrigerate until ready to use.

3. Place peppers and garlic in food processor; process until peppers are coarsely chopped. Add cilantro, lime juice, orange juice and pepper sauce; process until cilantro is finely chopped but mixture is not puréed.

4. Combine jicama, shrimp and tomato in large bowl. Add bell pepper mixture; toss to coat evenly. Serve over lettuce.

Nutrients per Serving: Calories 69; Total Fat 1g; Saturated Fat <1g; Protein 6g; Total Carbohydrates 10g; Fiber 1g; Cholesterol 42mg; Sodium 120mg

PORTOBELLO MUSHROOMS SESAME

MAKES 4 SERVINGS ✦ NET CARB COUNT: 9 GRAMS

4 large portobello mushrooms

2 tablespoons sweet rice wine

2 tablespoons reduced-sodium soy sauce

2 cloves garlic, minced

1 teaspoon dark sesame oil

1. Remove and discard stems from mushrooms; set caps aside. Combine remaining ingredients in small bowl.

2. Brush both sides of mushroom caps with soy sauce mixture. Grill mushrooms, top side up, on covered grill over medium coals 3 to 4 minutes. Brush tops with soy sauce mixture and turn over; grill 2 minutes more or until mushrooms are lightly browned. Turn again and grill, basting frequently, 4 to 5 minutes or until tender when pressed with back of spatula. Remove mushrooms and cut diagonally into ½-inch-thick slices.

Nutrients per Serving (1 grilled mushroom cap): Calories 67; Total Fat 2g; Saturated Fat <1g; Protein 4g; Total Carbohydrates 9g; Fiber <1g; Cholesterol 0; Sodium 268mg

SOUTHERN CRAB CAKES WITH RÉMOULADE DIPPING SAUCE

MAKES 8 SERVINGS ✦ NET CARB COUNT: 8 GRAMS

10   ounces fresh lump crabmeat

1½   cups fresh white or sourdough bread crumbs, divided

¼   cup chopped green onions

½   cup fat-free or reduced-fat mayonnaise, divided

1   egg white, lightly beaten

2   tablespoons coarse grain or spicy brown mustard, divided

¾   teaspoon hot pepper sauce, divided

2   teaspoons olive oil, divided

Lemon wedges

1. Preheat oven to 200°F. Combine crabmeat, ¾ cup bread crumbs and green onions in medium bowl. Add ¼ cup mayonnaise, egg white, 1 tablespoon mustard and ½ teaspoon pepper sauce; mix well. Using ¼ cup mixture per cake, shape eight ½-inch-thick cakes. Roll crab cakes lightly in remaining ¾ cup bread crumbs.

2. Heat large nonstick skillet over medium heat until hot; add 1 teaspoon oil. Add 4 crab cakes; cook 4 to 5 minutes per side or until golden brown. Transfer to serving platter; keep warm in oven. Repeat with remaining 1 teaspoon oil and crab cakes.

3. To prepare dipping sauce, combine remaining ¼ cup mayonnaise, 1 tablespoon mustard and ¼ teaspoon hot pepper sauce in small bowl; mix well.

4. Serve crab cakes warm with lemon wedges and dipping sauce.

Nutrients per Serving (1 crab cake with 1½ teaspoons dipping sauce): Calories 81; Total Fat 2g; Saturated Fat <1g; Protein 7g; Total Carbohydrates 8g; Fiber <1g; Cholesterol 30mg; Sodium 376mg

TURKEY HAM QUESADILLAS

MAKES 8 APPETIZER SERVINGS ✦ NET CARB COUNT: 10 GRAMS

¼ **cup picante sauce or salsa**

4 **(7-inch) regular or whole wheat flour tortillas**

½ **cup shredded reduced-fat reduced-sodium Monterey Jack cheese**

¼ **cup finely chopped turkey ham or lean ham**

¼ **cup canned diced green chilies, drained or 1 to 2 tablespoons chopped jalapeño peppers***

Nonstick cooking spray

Additional picante sauce or salsa for dipping (optional)

Fat-free or reduced-fat sour cream (optional)

*Jalapeño peppers can sting and irritate the skin; wear rubber gloves when handling peppers and do not touch eyes. Wash hands after handling.

1. Spread 1 tablespoon picante sauce on each tortilla.

2. Sprinkle cheese, turkey ham and chilies equally over half of each tortilla. Fold over uncovered half to make quesadilla; spray tops and bottoms of quesadillas with cooking spray.

3. Grill on uncovered grill over medium coals 1½ minutes per side or until cheese is melted and tortillas are golden brown, turning once. Quarter each quesadilla and serve with additional picante sauce and fat-free sour cream, if desired.

Nutrients per Serving (2 quesadillas): Calories 82; Total Fat 2g; Saturated Fat <1g; Protein 5g; Total Carbohydrates 11g; Fiber 1g; Cholesterol 5mg; Sodium 226mg

CHUNKY CHICKEN AND VEGETABLE SOUP

MAKES 4 SERVINGS ✦ NET CARB COUNT: 4 GRAMS

- 1 tablespoon canola oil
- 1 boneless skinless chicken breast (4 ounces), diced
- ½ cup chopped green bell pepper
- ½ cup thinly sliced celery
- 2 green onions, sliced
- 2 cans (14½ ounces each) chicken broth
- 1 cup water
- ½ cup sliced carrots
- 2 tablespoons cream
- 1 tablespoon finely chopped parsley
- ¼ teaspoon dried thyme leaves
- ⅛ teaspoon black pepper

1. Heat oil in large saucepan over medium heat. Add chicken; cook and stir 4 to 5 minutes or until no longer pink. Add bell pepper, celery and onions. Cook and stir 7 minutes or until vegetables are tender.

2. Add broth, water, carrots, cream, parsley, thyme and black pepper. Simmer 10 minutes or until carrots are tender.

Nutrients per Serving: Calories 130; Total Fat 8g; Saturated Fat 3g; Protein 9g; Total Carbohydrates 5g; Fiber 1g; Cholesterol 27mg; Sodium 895mg

SOUPS

ITALIAN SAUSAGE AND VEGETABLE STEW

MAKES 6 (1-CUP) SERVINGS ✦ NET CARB COUNT: 10 GRAMS

1 **pound hot or mild Italian sausage links, cut into 1-inch pieces**
1 **package (16 ounces) frozen vegetable blend, such as onions and green, red and yellow bell peppers**
2 **medium zucchini, sliced**
1 **can (14½ ounces) diced Italian-style tomatoes, undrained**
1 **jar (4½ ounces) sliced mushrooms, drained**
4 **cloves garlic, minced**

1. Cook sausage in large saucepan, covered, over medium to medium-high heat 5 minutes or until browned; pour off drippings.

2. Add frozen vegetables, zucchini, tomatoes with juice, mushrooms and garlic; bring to a boil. Reduce heat and simmer, covered, 10 minutes. Cook uncovered 5 to 10 minutes or until juices have thickened slightly

Nutrients per Serving (1 cup): Calories 234; Total Fat 15g; Saturated Fat 6g; Protein 14g; Total Carbohydrates 12g; Fiber 2g; Cholesterol 43mg; Sodium 732mg

SPICY PUMPKIN SOUP WITH GREEN CHILI SWIRL

MAKES 4 SERVINGS ✦ NET CARB COUNT: 8 GRAMS

1 **can (4 ounces) diced green chilies**

¼ **cup reduced-fat sour cream**

¼ **cup fresh cilantro leaves**

1 **can (15 ounces) solid-pack pumpkin**

1 **can (about 14 ounces) fat-free reduced-sodium chicken broth**

½ **cup water**

1 **teaspoon ground cumin**

½ **teaspoon chili powder**

¼ **teaspoon garlic powder**

⅛ **teaspoon ground red pepper (optional)**

Additional sour cream (optional)

1. Combine green chilies, ¼ cup sour cream and cilantro in food processor or blender; process until smooth.*

2. Combine pumpkin, chicken broth, water, cumin, chili powder, garlic powder and red pepper, if desired, in medium saucepan; stir in ¼ cup green chili mixture. Bring to a boil; reduce heat to medium. Simmer, uncovered, 5 minutes, stirring occasionally.

3. Pour into serving bowls. Top each serving with small dollops of remaining green chili mixture and additional sour cream, if desired. Run tip of spoon through dollops to swirl.

Omit food processor step by adding green chilies directly to soup. Finely chop cilantro and combine with sour cream. Dollop with sour cream-cilantro mixture as directed.

Nutrients per Serving: Calories 72; Total Fat 1g; Saturated Fat <1g; Protein 4g; Total Carbohydrates 12g; Fiber 4g; Cholesterol 5mg; Sodium 276mg

STIR-FRY BEEF & VEGETABLE SOUP

MAKES 6 SERVINGS ✦ NET CARB COUNT: 7 GRAMS

1 **boneless beef top sirloin or top round steak (about 1 pound)**
2 **teaspoons dark sesame oil, divided**
3 **cans (about 14 ounces each) reduced-sodium beef broth**
1 **package (16 ounces) frozen stir-fry vegetables**
3 **green onions, thinly sliced**
¼ **cup stir-fry sauce**

1. Slice beef lengthwise in half, then crosswise into ⅛-inch-thick strips.

2. Heat Dutch oven over high heat. Add 1 teaspoon sesame oil and tilt pan to coat bottom. Add half the beef in single layer; cook 1 minute, without stirring, until lightly browned on bottom. Turn and brown other side about 1 minute. Remove beef from pan; set aside. Repeat with remaining 1 teaspoon sesame oil and beef; set aside.

3. Add broth to Dutch oven; cover and bring to a boil over high heat. Add vegetables; reduce heat and simmer 3 to 5 minutes or until vegetables are heated through. Add beef, green onions and stir-fry sauce; simmer 1 minute.

Nutrients per Serving: Calories 159; Total Fat 5g; Saturated Fat 5g; Protein 20g; Total Carbohydrates 7g; Fiber <1g; Cholesterol 43mg; Sodium 356mg

THAI NOODLE SOUP

MAKES 4 SERVINGS ✦ NET CARB COUNT: 11 GRAMS

 1 **package (3 ounces) ramen noodles**
¾ **pound chicken tenders**
 2 **cans (about 14 ounces each) chicken broth**
¼ **cup shredded carrot**
¼ **cup frozen snow peas**
 2 **tablespoons thinly sliced green onion tops**
½ **teaspoon minced garlic**
¼ **teaspoon ground ginger**
 3 **tablespoons chopped fresh cilantro**
½ **lime, cut into 4 wedges**

1. Break noodles into pieces. Cook noodles according to package directions, discarding flavor packet. Drain and set aside.

2. Cut chicken tenders into ½-inch pieces. Combine chicken tenders and chicken broth in large saucepan or Dutch oven; bring to a boil over medium heat. Cook 2 minutes.

3. Add carrot, snow peas, green onion tops, garlic and ginger. Reduce heat to low; simmer 3 minutes. Add cooked noodles and cilantro; heat through. Serve soup with lime wedges.

Nutrients per Serving: Calories 200; Total Fat 7g; Saturated Fat 1g; Protein 23g; Total Carbohydrates 13g; Fiber 2g; Cholesterol 78mg; Sodium 900mg

CIOPPINO

MAKES 4 SERVINGS ✦ NET CARB COUNT: 6 GRAMS

- 1 teaspoon olive oil
- 1 large onion, chopped
- 1 cup sliced celery, with celery tops
- 1 clove garlic, minced
- 4 cups water
- 1 fish-flavored bouillon cube
- 1 tablespoon salt-free Italian herb seasoning
- ¼ pound cod or other boneless mild-flavored fish fillets
- 1 large tomato, chopped
- 1 can (10 ounces) baby clams, rinsed and drained (optional)
- ¼ pound uncooked small shrimp, peeled and deveined
- ¼ pound uncooked bay scallops
- ¼ cup flaked crabmeat or crabmeat blend
- 2 tablespoons fresh lemon juice

1. Heat olive oil in large saucepan over medium heat until hot. Add onion, celery and garlic. Cook and stir 5 minutes or until onion is soft. Add water, bouillon cube and Italian seasoning. Cover and bring to a boil over high heat.

2. Cut fish into ½-inch pieces. Add fish and tomato to saucepan. Reduce heat to medium-low; simmer about 5 minutes or until fish is opaque. Add clams, if desired, shrimp, scallops, crabmeat and lemon juice; simmer about 5 minutes or until shrimp and scallops are opaque.

Nutrients per Serving (1¾ cups): Calories 122; Total Fat 2g; Saturated Fat <1g; Protein 18g; Total Carbohydrates 8g; Fiber 2g; Cholesterol 75mg; Sodium 412mg

SOUPS

HOT AND SOUR SOUP

MAKES 7 (1-CUP) SERVINGS ✦ NET CARB COUNT: 6 GRAMS

 3 **cans (about 14 ounces each) chicken broth**
 8 **ounces boneless skinless chicken breasts, cut into ¼-inch-thick strips**
 1 **cup shredded carrots**
 1 **cup thinly sliced mushrooms**
 ½ **cup bamboo shoots, cut into matchstick-size strips**
 2 **tablespoons rice vinegar or white wine vinegar**
 ½ **to ¾ teaspoon white pepper**
 ¼ **to ½ teaspoon hot pepper sauce**
 2 **tablespoons cornstarch**
 2 **tablespoons soy sauce**
 1 **tablespoon dry sherry**
 2 **medium green onions, sliced**
 1 **egg, lightly beaten**

1. Combine chicken broth, chicken, carrots, mushrooms, bamboo shoots, vinegar, pepper and hot pepper sauce in large saucepan. Bring to a boil over medium-high heat; reduce heat to low. Cover and simmer about 5 minutes or until chicken is no longer pink.

2. Stir together cornstarch, soy sauce and sherry in small bowl until smooth. Add to chicken broth mixture. Cook and stir until mixture comes to a boil. Stir in green onions and egg. Cook about 1 minute, stirring in one direction, until egg is cooked. Ladle soup into bowls.

Nutrients per Serving: (1 cup): Calories 85; Total Fat 2g; Saturated Fat 1g; Protein 8g; Total Carbohydrates 7g; Fiber 1g; Cholesterol 43mg; Sodium 1,031mg

MEDITERRANEAN SHRIMP SOUP

MAKES 6 SERVINGS ✦ NET CARB COUNT: 10 GRAMS

- 2 cans (14½ ounces each) reduced-sodium chicken broth
- 1 can (14½ ounces) diced tomatoes, undrained
- 1 can (8 ounces) tomato sauce
- 1 medium onion, chopped
- ½ medium green bell pepper, chopped
- ½ cup orange juice
- ½ cup dry white wine (optional)
- 1 jar (2½ ounces) sliced mushrooms
- ¼ cup ripe olives, sliced
- 2 cloves garlic, minced
- 1 teaspoon dried basil leaves
- 2 bay leaves
- ¼ teaspoon fennel seeds, crushed
- ⅛ teaspoon black pepper
- 1 pound medium shrimp, peeled

Slow Cooker Directions

Place all ingredients except shrimp in slow cooker. Cover; cook on LOW 4 to 4½ hours or until vegetables are crisp-tender. Stir in shrimp. Cover; cook 15 to 30 minutes or until shrimp are opaque. Remove and discard bay leaves.

Note: For a heartier soup, add some fish. Cut 1 pound of whitefish or cod into 1-inch pieces. Add the fish to the slow cooker 45 minutes before serving. Cover and cook on LOW.

Nutrients per Serving: Calories 162; Total Fat 3g; Saturated Fat <1g; Protein 21g; Total Carbohydrates 12g; Fiber 2g; Cholesterol 129mg; Sodium 678mg

MEXICAN TORTILLA SOUP

MAKES 8 SERVINGS ✦ NET CARB COUNT: 12 GRAMS

   Nonstick cooking spray
2 pounds boneless skinless chicken breasts, cut into ½-inch cubes
4 cups diced carrots
2 cups sliced celery
1 cup chopped green bell pepper
1 cup chopped onion
4 cloves garlic, minced
1 jalapeño pepper,* seeded and sliced
1 teaspoon dried oregano leaves
½ teaspoon ground cumin
8 cups fat-free reduced-sodium chicken broth
1 large tomato, seeded and chopped
4 to 5 tablespoons lime juice
2 (6-inch) corn tortillas, cut into ¼-inch strips
   Salt (optional)
3 tablespoons finely chopped fresh cilantro

Jalapeño peppers can sting and irritate the skin; wear rubber gloves when handling peppers and do not touch eyes. Wash hands after handling.

1. Preheat oven to 350°F. Spray large nonstick Dutch oven with cooking spray; heat over medium heat. Add chicken; cook and stir about 10 minutes or until browned and no longer pink in center. Add carrots, celery, bell pepper, onion, garlic, jalapeño pepper, oregano and cumin; cook and stir over medium heat 5 minutes.

2. Stir in chicken broth, tomato and lime juice; heat to a boil. Reduce heat to low; cover and simmer 15 to 20 minutes.

3. Meanwhile, spray tortilla strips lightly with cooking spray; sprinkle very lightly with salt, if desired. Place on baking sheet. Bake about 10 minutes or until browned and crisp, stirring occasionally.

4. Stir cilantro into soup. Ladle soup into bowls; top evenly with tortilla strips.

Nutrients per Serving (1¾ cup soup with tortilla strips): Calories 184; Total Fat 3g; Saturated Fat <1g; Protein 23g; Total Carbohydrates 16g; Fiber 4g; Cholesterol 58mg; Sodium 132mg

SOUPS

POZOLE

MAKES 6 SERVINGS ✦ NET CARB COUNT: 12 GRAMS

 1 **large onion, thinly sliced**

 1 **tablespoon olive oil**

 2 **teaspoons dried oregano leaves**

 1 **clove garlic, minced**

 ½ **teaspoon ground cumin**

 2 **cans (about 14 ounces each) chicken broth**

 1 **package (10 ounces) frozen corn**

 1 to 2 **cans (4 ounces each) chopped green chilies, undrained**

 1 **can (2¼ ounces) sliced ripe olives, drained**

 ¾ **pound boneless skinless chicken breasts**

1. Combine onion, oil, oregano, garlic and cumin in Dutch oven. Cover and cook over medium heat about 6 minutes or until onion is tender, stirring occasionally.

2. Stir broth, corn, chilies and olives into onion mixture. Cover and bring to a boil over high heat.

3. While soup is cooking, cut chicken into thin strips. Add to soup. Reduce heat to medium-low; cover and cook 3 to 4 minutes or until chicken is no longer pink.

Hint: Sprinkle Pozole with chopped fresh cilantro before serving.

Nutrients per Serving: Calories 193; Total Fat 8g; Saturated Fat <1g; Protein 16g; Total Carbohydrates 15g; Fiber 3g; Cholesterol 41mg; Sodium 990mg

ROAST CHICKEN WITH PEPPERS

MAKES 6 SERVINGS ✦ NET CARB COUNT: 4 GRAMS

1 **chicken (3 to 3½ pounds), cut into pieces**

3 **tablespoons olive oil, divided**

1½ **tablespoons chopped fresh rosemary or 1½ teaspoons dried rosemary, crushed**

1 **tablespoon fresh lemon juice**

1¼ **teaspoons salt, divided**

¾ **teaspoon freshly ground black pepper, divided**

3 **bell peppers (preferably 1 red, 1 yellow and 1 green)**

1 **medium onion**

1. Preheat oven to 375°F. Rinse chicken in cold water; pat dry with paper towels. Place in shallow roasting pan.

2. Combine 2 tablespoons oil, rosemary and lemon juice; brush over chicken. Sprinkle 1 teaspoon salt and ½ teaspoon pepper over chicken. Roast 15 minutes.

3. Cut bell peppers lengthwise into ½-inch-thick strips. Slice onion into thin wedges. Toss vegetables with remaining 1 tablespoon oil, ¼ teaspoon salt and ¼ teaspoon pepper. Spoon vegetables around chicken; roast about 40 minutes or until vegetables are tender and chicken is no longer pink in center. Serve chicken with vegetables and pan juices.

Nutrients per Serving: Calories 428; Total Fat 32g; Saturated Fat 8g; Protein 29g; Total Carbohydrates 6g; Fiber 2g; Cholesterol 118mg; Sodium 575mg

PARMESAN TURKEY BREAST

MAKES 4 SERVINGS ✦ NET CARB COUNT: 3 GRAMS

½ **teaspoon salt**

¼ **teaspoon freshly ground black pepper**

1 **pound turkey breast, chicken breast or veal cutlets, cut ⅛- to ¼-inch thick**

2 **tablespoons butter, melted**

2 **cloves garlic, minced, or 1 teaspoon bottled minced garlic**

½ **cup grated Parmesan cheese**

1 **cup spicy marinara sauce or mushroom or olive pasta sauce, warmed**

2 **tablespoons chopped fresh basil or Italian parsley**

Preheat broiler. Sprinkle salt and pepper over turkey. Place turkey in 1 layer in a 15×10-inch jellyroll pan. Combine butter and garlic; brush over turkey. Broil 4 to 5 inches from heat source for 2 minutes; turn. Top with cheese. Continue to broil 2 to 3 minutes or until turkey is no longer pink in center. Transfer to serving plates; spoon sauce over turkey and top with basil.

Variation: Preheat oven to 350°F. Sprinkle salt and pepper over turkey. Brown turkey on both sides in 1 to 2 tablespoons hot oil in a medium skillet. Place browned turkey in a small casserole or 9×9-inch baking dish. Top with pasta sauce, cover pan with foil, and bake about 30 minutes or until no longer pink in center. Remove from oven and remove foil; sprinkle with Parmesan cheese and basil.

Nutrients per Serving (¼ pound turkey plus ¼ cup sauce and ½ tablespoon basil): Calories 251; Total Fat 10g; Saturated Fat 6g; Protein 33g; Total Carbohydrates 5g; Fiber 2g; Cholesterol 95mg; Sodium 832mg

BLUE CHEESE-STUFFED SIRLOIN PATTIES

MAKES 4 SERVINGS ✦ NET CARB COUNT: 2 GRAMS

- 1½ **pounds ground beef sirloin**
- ½ **cup (2 ounces) shredded sharp Cheddar cheese**
- ¼ **cup crumbled blue cheese**
- ¼ **cup finely chopped parsley**
- 2 **teaspoons Dijon mustard**
- 1 **teaspoon Worcestershire sauce**
- 1 **clove garlic, minced**
- ¼ **teaspoon salt, plus more to taste**
- 2 **teaspoons olive oil**
- 1 **medium red bell pepper, cut into thin strips**

1. Shape beef into 8 patties, about 4 inches in diameter and ¼ inch thick.

2. Combine cheeses, parsley, mustard, Worcestershire sauce, garlic and ¼ teaspoon salt in small bowl; toss gently to blend.

3. Mound ¼ cheese mixture on each of 4 patties (about 3 tablespoons per patty). Top with remaining 4 patties; pinch edges of patties to seal completely. Set aside.

4. Heat oil in 12-inch nonstick skillet over medium-high heat until hot. Add pepper strips; cook and stir until edges of peppers begin to brown. Sprinkle with salt to taste. Remove from skillet and keep warm.

5. Add beef patties to same skillet; cook on medium-high 5 minutes. Turn patties; top with peppers. Cook 4 minutes or until patties are no longer pink in centers (160°F).

Nutrients per Serving: Calories 463; Total Fat 32g; Saturated Fat 16g; Protein 38g; Total Carbohydrates 3g; Fiber 1g; Cholesterol 131mg; Sodium 548mg

STEAKS WITH ZESTY MERLOT SAUCE

MAKES 4 SERVINGS ✦ NET CARB COUNT: 4 GRAMS

½ cup **Merlot wine**

2 tablespoons **Worcestershire sauce**

1 tablespoon **balsamic vinegar**

1 teaspoon **sugar**

1 teaspoon **beef bouillon granules**

½ teaspoon **dried thyme leaves**

2 beef **ribeye steaks (8 ounces each)**

2 tablespoons **finely chopped parsley**

1. Combine wine, Worcestershire sauce, vinegar, sugar, bouillon granules and thyme; set aside.

2. Heat large nonstick skillet over high heat until hot. Add steaks; cook 3 minutes on each side. Turn steaks again and cook 3 to 6 minutes longer over medium heat or until desired doneness.

3. Cut steaks in half; arrange on serving platter. Place in oven to keep warm.

4. Add wine mixture to same skillet. Bring to a boil; cook and stir 1 minute, scraping up any brown bits. Spoon over steaks. Sprinkle with parsley; serve immediately.

Nutrients per Serving: Calories 287; Total Fat 17g; Saturated Fat 5g; Protein 23g; Total Carbohydrates 4g; Fiber <1g; Cholesterol 58mg; Sodium 294mg

SIRLOIN WITH SWEET CARAMELIZED ONIONS

MAKES 4 SERVINGS ✦ NET CARB COUNT: 6 GRAMS

   Nonstick cooking spray
1 **medium onion, very thinly sliced**
1 **boneless beef top sirloin steak (about 1 pound)**
¼ **cup water**
2 **tablespoons Worcestershire sauce**
1 **tablespoon sugar**

1. Lightly coat 12-inch skillet with cooking spray; heat over high heat until hot. Add onion; cook and stir 4 minutes or until browned. Remove from skillet and set aside. Wipe out skillet with paper towel.

2. Coat same skillet with cooking spray; heat until hot. Add beef; cook 10 to 13 minutes for medium-rare to medium, turning once. Remove from heat and transfer to cutting board; let stand 3 minutes before slicing.

3. Meanwhile, return skillet to high heat until hot; add onion, water, Worcestershire sauce and sugar. Cook 30 to 45 seconds or until most liquid has evaporated.

4. Thinly slice beef on the diagonal and serve with onions.

Nutrients per Serving: Calories 159; Total Fat 5g; Saturated Fat 2g; Protein 21g; Total Carbohydrates 7g; Fiber 1g; Cholesterol 60mg; Sodium 118mg

LOW-CARB LASAGNA

MAKES 16 SERVINGS ✦ NET CARB COUNT: 6 GRAMS

  2 **medium eggplants (about 1½ pounds total)**
  1 **tablespoon salt plus 1 teaspoon salt, divided**
1½ **pounds ground beef**
1½ **cups meatless pasta sauce (8 or less grams of carbohydrate per ½ cup)***
  1 **teaspoon Italian seasoning**
 ½ **teaspoon garlic powder**
 ½ **teaspoon pepper**
  4 **cups (2 pounds) whole milk ricotta cheese**
  1 **egg**
  3 **tablespoons chopped parsley, divided**
  2 **cups (8 ounces) shredded mozzarella cheese**
 ¼ **cup grated Parmesan cheese**

*Check labels carefully. Carbohydrate counts vary greatly.

1. Preheat oven to 350°F. Oil 12×8-inch baking pan. Slice eggplant horizontally into ⅛-inch thick pieces. Layer slices in colander, sprinkling with 1 tablespoon salt. Set aside to drain for at least 20 minutes.

2. Meanwhile, cook ground beef in large skillet until no longer pink. Drain fat. Add pasta sauce, Italian seasoning, remaining 1 teaspoon salt, garlic powder and pepper; cook and stir 5 minutes to blend flavors.

3. Spoon ricotta into large bowl. Add egg. With electric mixer beat until light. Mix in 2 tablespoons parsley.

4. Rinse eggplant slices and dry on paper towels. Arrange single layer of eggplant slices in prepared pan. Layer with ½ of ricotta mixture, ½ of meat sauce, ½ of mozzarella and ½ of Parmesan. Arrange eggplant slices over top and layer with remaining ½ of ricotta mixture and ½ of meat sauce. Top with remaining eggplant slices, remaining mozzarella and Parmesan. Sprinkle top with remaining 1 tablespoon parsley.

5. Bake 30 minutes uncovered. Tent loosely with foil and bake an additional 10 minutes or until lasagna is heated through and sauce is bubbly.

Nutrients per Serving: Calories 295; Total Fat 20g; Saturated Fat 10g; Protein 20g; Total Carbohydrates 9; Fiber 3g; Cholesterol 86mg; Sodium 463mg

SOUTHWEST SPAGHETTI SQUASH

MAKES 4 SERVINGS ✦ NET CARB COUNT: 12 GRAMS

- **1 spaghetti squash (about 3 pounds)**
- **1 can (about 14 ounces) Mexican-style diced tomatoes, undrained**
- **1 can (about 14 ounces) black beans, rinsed and drained**
- **¾ cup (3 ounces) shredded Monterey Jack cheese, divided**
- **¼ cup finely chopped cilantro**
- **1 teaspoon ground cumin**
- **¼ teaspoon garlic salt**
- **¼ teaspoon black pepper**

1. Preheat oven to 350°F. Cut squash in half lengthwise. Remove and discard seeds. Place squash, cut side down, in greased baking pan. Bake 45 minutes to 1 hour or until just tender. Using fork, remove spaghetti-like strands from hot squash and place strands in large bowl. (Use oven mitts to protect hands.)

2. Add tomatoes with juice, beans, ½ cup cheese, cilantro, cumin, garlic salt and pepper; toss well.

3. Spray 1½-quart casserole with nonstick cooking spray. Spoon mixture into casserole. Sprinkle with remaining ¼ cup cheese.

4. Bake, uncovered, 30 to 35 minutes or until heated through. Serve immediately.

Nutrients per Serving (1⅓ cups): Calories 147; Total Fat 5g; Saturated Fat 3g; Protein 8g; Total Carbohydrates 18; Fiber 6g; Cholesterol 13mg; Sodium 609mg

MAIN DISHES

MAIN DISHES

PORK KABOBS IN MARGARITA MARINADE

MAKES 4 SERVINGS ✦ NET CARB COUNT: 12 GRAMS

Marinade

- 1 **cup lime juice**
- 4 **teaspoons sugar**
- ½ **teaspoon salt**
- 1 **teaspoon ground coriander or 1 tablespoon minced cilantro**
- 1 **clove garlic, minced**

- 1 **pound pork tenderloin, cut into 1½-inch cubes**
- ¼ **cup butter, melted**
- 1 **tablespoon lime juice or to taste**
- 1 **medium green bell pepper, cut into 1½-inch cubes**
- 1 **medium red bell pepper, cut into 1½-inch cubes**
- 2 **ears corn, cut into 8 pieces**

1. In a small bowl, mix 1 cup lime juice, 4 teaspoons sugar, ½ teaspoon salt, coriander and garlic; set aside. Place pork in large resealable plastic bag; pour marinade over pork. Seal bag and refrigerate about 45 minutes. If using bamboo skewers, soak in enough water to cover for at least 30 minutes before using to prevent burning.

2. Combine butter and 1 tablespoon lime juice in small bowl; set aside.

3. Remove pork from marinade; drain. Discard marinade. Evenly thread pork, bell pepper and corn onto skewers. Grill over hot coals 15 minutes or just until no longer pink in center, basting with butter mixture and turning frequently. Or, broil in preheated broiler, basting and turning frequently, until pork is no longer pink in center.

Nutrients per Serving: Calories 240; Total Fat 10g; Saturated Fat 3g; Protein 25g; Total Carbohydrates 13g; Fiber 1g; Cholesterol 66mg; Sodium 129mg

SPINACH, CHEESE AND PROSCIUTTO-STUFFED CHICKEN BREASTS

MAKES 4 SERVINGS ✦ NET CARB COUNT: 7 GRAMS

4 boneless skinless chicken breasts (about 4 ounces each)
   Salt and black pepper
4 slices (½ ounce each) prosciutto*
4 slices (½ ounce each) smoked provolone
1 cup spinach leaves, chopped
4 tablespoons all-purpose flour, divided
1 tablespoon olive oil
1 tablespoon butter
1 cup chicken broth
1 tablespoon heavy cream

Prosciutto, an Italian ham, is seasoned, cured and air-dried, not smoked. Look for imported or less expensive domestic prosciutto in delis and Italian food markets.

1. Preheat oven to 350°F. To form pocket, cut each chicken breast horizontally almost to opposite edge. Fold back top half of chicken breast; sprinkle chicken lightly with salt and pepper. Place 1 slice prosciutto, 1 slice provolone and ¼ cup spinach on each chicken breast. Fold top half of breasts over filling.

2. Spread 3 tablespoons flour on plate. Holding chicken breast closed, coat with flour; shake off excess. Lightly sprinkle chicken with salt and pepper.

3. Heat oil and butter in large skillet over medium heat. Place chicken in skillet; cook about 4 minutes on each side or until browned.

4. Transfer chicken to shallow baking dish. Bake 10 minutes or until chicken is no longer pink in center and juices run clear.

5. Whisk chicken broth and cream into remaining 1 tablespoon flour in small bowl. Pour chicken broth mixture into same skillet; heat over medium heat, stirring constantly, until sauce thickens, about 3 minutes. Spoon sauce onto serving plates; top with chicken breasts.

Tip: Swiss, Gruyére or mozzarella cheese may be substituted for the smoked provolone. Thinly sliced deli ham can be substituted for the prosciutto.

Nutrients per Serving: Calories 371; Total Fat 23g; Saturated Fat 9g; Protein 33g; Total Carbohydrates 7g; Fiber <1g; Cholesterol 105mg; Sodium 854mg

ROAST TURKEY BREAST WITH SPINACH-BLUE CHEESE STUFFING

MAKES 14 SERVINGS ✦ NET CARB COUNT: 1 GRAM

1   **frozen whole boneless turkey breast, thawed (3½ to 4 pounds)**

1   **package (10 ounces) frozen chopped spinach, thawed and squeezed dry**

2   **ounces blue cheese or feta cheese**

2   **ounces reduced-fat cream cheese**

½   **cup finely chopped green onions**

4½   **teaspoons Dijon mustard**

4½   **teaspoons dried basil leaves**

2   **teaspoons dried oregano leaves**

    Black pepper to taste

    Paprika

1. Preheat oven to 350°F. Coat roasting pan and rack with nonstick cooking spray.

2. Unroll turkey breast; rinse and pat dry. Place between 2 sheets of plastic wrap. Pound turkey breast with flat side of meat mallet to about 1-inch thickness. Remove and discard skin from ½ of turkey breast; turn meat over so skin side (on other half) faces down.

3. Combine spinach, blue cheese, cream cheese, green onions, mustard, basil and oregano in medium bowl; mix well. Spread evenly over turkey breast. Roll up turkey so skin is on top.

4. Carefully place turkey breast on rack; sprinkle with pepper and paprika. Roast 1½ hours or until no longer pink in center of breast. Remove from oven and let stand 10 minutes before removing skin and slicing. Cut into 14 (¼-inch-thick) slices.

Nutrients per Serving (1 slice): Calories 135; Total Fat 4g; Saturated Fat 2g; Protein 22g; Total Carbohydrates 2g; Fiber 1g; Cholesterol 50mg; Sodium 144mg

PECAN CATFISH WITH CRANBERRY COMPOTE

MAKES 4 SERVINGS ✦ NET CARB COUNT: 12 GRAMS

1½ **cup pecans**

  2 **tablespoons flour**

  1 **egg**

  2 **tablespoons water**

  4 **catfish fillets (about 1¼ pounds)**

   Salt and pepper

  2 **tablespoons butter, divided**

   Cranberry Compote (recipe follows)

1. Preheat oven to 425°F. Place pecans and flour in bowl of food processor; pulse until finely chopped. (Do not overprocess or you may create nut butter.)

2. Place pecan mixture in shallow dish or plate; whisk egg and water in another shallow dish. Salt and pepper both sides of each fillet and dip first in egg mixture, then in pecan mixture, pressing to make pecans stick. Meanwhile, prepare baking pan: Place 1 tablespoon butter in 13×9-inch pan. Melt butter on stovetop or in oven and tilt to distribute evenly.

3. Place fillets in single layer in prepared pan. Top with pieces of remaining butter. Bake 15 to 20 minutes or until fish begins to flake when tested with fork. Serve with Cranberry Compote.

Cranberry Compote

  1 **bag (12 ounces) cranberries**

  ½ **cup orange juice**

  ¾ **cup water**

  ½ **cup sucralose-based sugar substitute**

  2 **tablespoons dark brown sugar**

  ¼ **teaspoon five-spice powder**

  2 **teaspoons grated fresh ginger**

  ⅛ **teaspoon salt**

  1 **teaspoon butter**

1. Wash and pick over cranberries, discarding any bad ones. Combine cranberries and all remaining ingredients except butter in large saucepan. Heat over medium-high heat, stirring occasionally, about 10 minutes or until berries begin to pop.

2. Cook and stir 5 minutes or until saucy consistency is reached. Remove from heat; stir in butter. Allow to cool; refrigerate until cold. Compote keeps up to 1 week under refrigeration.

Makes 4 cups

Nutrients per Serving (1 fillet plus ½ cup compote): Calories 305; Total Fat 21g; Saturated Fat 4g; Protein 16g; Total Carbohydrates 16g; Fiber 4g; Cholesterol 101mg; Sodium 97mg

QUICK ORANGE CHICKEN

MAKES 4 SERVINGS ✦ NET CARB COUNT: 9 GRAMS

2 **tablespoons frozen orange juice concentrate**

1 **tablespoon no-sugar-added orange marmalade**

1 **teaspoon Dijon mustard**

¼ **teaspoon salt**

4 **boneless skinless chicken breasts (about 1 pound)**

½ **cup fresh orange sections**

2 **tablespoons chopped fresh parsley**

1. For sauce, combine juice concentrate, marmalade, mustard and salt in 8-inch shallow round microwavable dish until juice concentrate is thawed.

2. Add chicken, coating both sides with sauce. Arrange chicken around edge of dish without overlapping. Cover with vented plastic wrap. Microwave at HIGH (100%) 3 minutes; turn chicken over. Microwave at MEDIUM-HIGH (70% power) 4 minutes or until chicken is no longer pink in center.

3. Remove chicken to serving plate. Microwave remaining sauce at HIGH (100%) 2 to 3 minutes or until slightly thickened.

4. To serve, spoon sauce over chicken; top with orange sections and parsley.

Nutrients per Serving: Calories 157; Total Fat 3g; Saturated Fat 1g; Protein 23g; Total Carbohydrates 10g; Fiber 1g; Cholesterol 60mg; Sodium 207mg

MAIN DISHES

GRILLED PORK TENDERLOIN MEDALLIONS

MAKES 4 SERVINGS ✦ NET CARB COUNT: 3 GRAMS

Pepper & Herb Rub

- 1 tablespoon garlic salt
- 1 tablespoon dried basil leaves
- 1 tablespoon dried thyme leaves
- 1½ teaspoons cracked black pepper
- 1½ teaspoons dried rosemary
- 1 teaspoon paprika

Pork

- 2 tablespoons Pepper & Herb Rub
- 12 pork tenderloin medallions (about 1 pound)
  Olive oil-flavored nonstick cooking spray

1. For rub, combine garlic salt, basil, thyme, pepper, rosemary and paprika in small jar or resealable plastic food storage bag. Store in cool dry place up to 3 months.

2. Prepare grill for direct cooking. Sprinkle rub evenly over both sides of pork; pressing lightly. Spray pork with cooking spray.

3. Place pork on grid over medium-hot coals. Grill, uncovered, 4 to 5 minutes per side or until pork is no longer pink in center.

Nutrients per Serving (3 medallions): Calories 42; Total Fat 12g; Saturated Fat 3g; Protein 72g; Total Carbohydrates 6g; Fiber 3g; Cholesterol 198mg; Sodium 1,584mg

MAIN DISHES

MESQUITE-GRILLED SALMON FILLETS

MAKES 4 SERVINGS ✦ NET CARB COUNT: I GRAM

2 **tablespoons olive oil**

I **clove garlic, minced**

2 **tablespoons lemon juice**

I **teaspoon grated lemon peel**

½ **teaspoon dried dill weed**

½ **teaspoon dried thyme leaves**

¼ **teaspoon salt**

¼ **teaspoon black pepper**

4 **salmon fillets, ¾ to I inch thick (about 5 ounces each)**

1. Cover I cup mesquite chips with cold water; soak 20 to 30 minutes. Prepare grill for direct cooking.

2. Combine oil and garlic in small microwavable bowl. Microwave at HIGH I minute or until garlic is tender. Add lemon juice, lemon peel, dill, thyme, salt and pepper; whisk until blended. Brush skinless sides of salmon with half of lemon mixture.

3. Drain mesquite chips; sprinkle chips over coals. Place salmon, skin side up, on grid. Grill, covered, over medium-high heat 4 to 5 minutes; turn and brush with remaining lemon mixture. Grill 4 to 5 minutes or until salmon flakes easily when tested with fork.

Nutrients per Serving: Calories 225; Total Fat 12g; Saturated Fat 2g; Protein 28g; Total Carbohydrates 1g; Fiber trace; Cholesterol 72mg; Sodium 226mg

MOROCCAN-STYLE LAMB CHOPS

MAKES 4 SERVINGS ✦ NET CARB COUNT: <1 GRAM

- 1 **teaspoon ground cumin**
- 1 **teaspoon ground coriander**
- ¾ **teaspoon salt**
- ⅛ **teaspoon cinnamon**
- ⅛ **teaspoon cayenne pepper**
- 1 **tablespoon olive oil**
- 4 **center cut loin lamb chops, cut 1-inch thick (about 1 pound)**
- 2 **cloves garlic, minced**

Prepare grill or preheat broiler. In a cup or small bowl, combine cumin, coriander, salt, cinnamon, cayenne pepper and oil; mix well. Rub or brush oil-spice mixture over both sides of lamb chops. Sprinkle garlic over both sides of lamb chops. Grill on a covered grill or broil 4 to 5 inches from heat source 4 minutes per side for medium-rare or 5 minutes per side for medium.

Tip: This recipe works well on an indoor, electric, countertop grill.

Nutrients per Serving: Calories 173; Total Fat 8g; Saturated Fat 2g; Protein 23g; Total Carbohydrates <1g; Fiber trace; Cholesterol 71mg; Sodium 510mg

GRILLED SALMON FILLETS, ASPARAGUS AND ONIONS

MAKES 6 SERVINGS ✦ NET CARB COUNT: 6 GRAMS

½ teaspoon paprika

6 salmon fillets (6 to 8 ounces each)

⅓ cup bottled honey-Dijon marinade or barbecue sauce

1 bunch (about 1 pound) fresh asparagus spears, ends trimmed

1 large red or sweet onion, cut into ¼-inch slices

1 tablespoon olive oil

Salt and black pepper

1. Prepare grill for direct grilling. Sprinkle paprika over salmon fillets. Brush marinade over salmon; let stand at room temperature 15 minutes.

2. Brush asparagus and onion slices with olive oil; season to taste with salt and pepper.

3. Place salmon, skin side down, in center of grid over medium coals. Arrange asparagus spears and onion slices around salmon. Grill salmon and vegetables on covered grill 5 minutes. Turn salmon, asparagus and onion slices. Grill 5 to 6 minutes more or until salmon flakes easily when tested with a fork and vegetables are crisp-tender. Separate onion slices into rings; arrange over asparagus.

Nutrients per Serving: Calories 255; Total Fat 8g; Saturated Fat 1g; Protein 35g; Total Carbohydrates 8g; Fiber 2g; Cholesterol 86mg; Sodium 483mg

SWEET-SOUR TURNIP GREEN SALAD

MAKES 4 SERVINGS ✦ NET CARB COUNT: 8 GRAMS

2 **cups shredded stemmed washed turnip greens**

2 **cups washed mixed salad greens**

1 **cup sliced plum tomatoes or quartered cherry tomatoes**

½ **cup shredded carrot**

⅓ **cup sliced green onions**

8 **tablespoons water, divided**

2 **teaspoons all-purpose flour**

1 **tablespoon packed brown sugar**

½ **teaspoon celery seeds**

Dash black pepper

1 **tablespoon white wine vinegar**

1. Combine turnip greens, salad greens, tomatoes and carrot in salad bowl; set aside. Combine green onions and 2 tablespoons water in small saucepan. Bring to a boil over high heat. Reduce heat to medium. Cook, covered, 2 to 3 minutes or until onions are tender.

2. Mix remaining 6 tablespoons water and flour in small bowl until smooth. Stir into green onions in saucepan. Add brown sugar, celery seeds and pepper; cook and stir until mixture boils and thickens. Cook and stir 1 minute more. Stir in vinegar. Pour hot dressing over salad; toss to coat. Serve immediately.

Nutrients per Serving: Calories 49; Total Fat <1g; Saturated Fat <1g; Protein 2g; Total Carbohydrates 11g; Fiber 3g; Cholesterol 0; Sodium 41mg

INDIAN-STYLE VEGETABLE STIR-FRY

MAKES 6 SERVINGS ✦ NET CARB COUNT: 6 GRAMS

1 teaspoon canola oil

1 teaspoon curry powder

1 teaspoon ground cumin

⅛ teaspoon red pepper flakes

1½ teaspoons minced seeded jalapeño pepper*

2 cloves garlic, minced

¾ cup chopped red bell pepper

¾ cup thinly sliced carrots

3 cups cauliflower florets

½ cup water, divided

½ teaspoon salt

2 teaspoons finely chopped fresh cilantro (optional)

Jalapeño peppers can sting and irritate the skin; wear rubber gloves when handling peppers and do not touch eyes. Wash hands after handling.

1. Heat oil in large nonstick skillet over medium-high heat. Add curry powder, cumin and red pepper flakes; cook and stir about 30 seconds.

2. Stir in jalapeño pepper and garlic. Add bell pepper and carrots; mix well. Add cauliflower; reduce heat to medium.

3. Stir in ¼ cup water; cook and stir until water evaporates. Add remaining ¼ cup water; cover and cook about 8 to 10 minutes or until vegetables are crisp-tender, stirring occasionally.

4. Add salt; mix well. Sprinkle with cilantro and garnish with mizuna and additional red bell pepper, if desired.

Nutrients per Serving (⅔ cup): Calories 40; Total Fat 1g; Saturated Fat <1g; Protein 2g; Total Carbohydrates 7g; Fiber 1g; Cholesterol 0; Sodium 198mg

ROASTED RED PEPPER & TOMATO CASSEROLE

MAKES 6 SERVINGS ✦ NET CARB COUNT: 8 GRAMS

1 jar (12 ounces) roasted red peppers, drained

1½ teaspoons red wine vinegar

1 teaspoon olive oil

1 clove garlic, minced

¼ teaspoon salt

¼ teaspoon black pepper

⅓ cup grated Parmesan cheese, divided

3 medium tomatoes (about 1½ pounds), sliced

½ cup (about 1 ounce) herb-flavored croutons, crushed

Microwave Directions

1. Combine red peppers, vinegar, oil, garlic, salt and black pepper in food processor; process, using on/off pulsing action, 1 minute or until slightly chunky. Reserve 2 tablespoons cheese for garnish. Stir remaining cheese into red pepper mixture.

2. Arrange tomato slices in 8-inch round microwavable baking dish; microwave at HIGH 1 minute. Spoon red pepper mixture on top; microwave at HIGH 2 to 3 minutes or until tomatoes are slightly soft.

3. Sprinkle with reserved cheese and croutons. Garnish, if desired.

Nutrients per Serving: Calories 80; Total Fat 2g; Saturated Fat 1g; Protein 3g; Total Carbohydrates 9g; Fiber 1g; Cholesterol 3mg; Sodium 342mg

SANTA FE GRILLED VEGETABLE SALAD

MAKES 8 SERVINGS ✦ NET CARB COUNT: 10 GRAMS

2 baby eggplants (6 ounces each), halved

1 medium yellow summer squash, halved

1 medium zucchini, halved

1 green bell pepper, cored and quartered

1 red bell pepper, cored and quartered

1 small onion, peeled and halved

½ cup orange juice

2 tablespoons lime juice

1 tablespoon olive oil

2 cloves garlic, minced

1 teaspoon dried oregano leaves

¼ teaspoon black pepper

¼ teaspoon ground red pepper

¼ teaspoon salt

2 tablespoons chopped fresh cilantro

1. Combine all ingredients except cilantro in large bowl; toss to coat.

2. To prevent sticking, spray grid with nonstick cooking spray. Prepare coals for direct grilling. Place vegetables on grill, 2 to 3 inches from hot coals; reserve marinade. Grill 3 to 4 minutes per side or until tender and lightly charred; cool 10 minutes. Or, place vegetables on rack of broiler pan coated with nonstick cooking spray; reserve marinade. Broil 2 to 3 inches from heat, 3 to 4 minutes per side or until tender; cool 10 minutes.

3. Remove peel from eggplant, if desired. Slice vegetables into bite-size pieces; return to marinade. Stir in cilantro; toss to coat.

Nutrients per Serving (1 cup): Calories 63; Total Fat 2g; Saturated Fat <1g; Protein 2g; Total Carbohydrates 11g; Fiber 1g; Cholesterol 0; Sodium 70mg

BROCCOLI WITH CREAMY LEMON SAUCE

MAKES 2 SERVINGS ✦ NET CARB COUNT: 5 GRAMS

- **2 tablespoons fat-free mayonnaise**
- **4½ teaspoons reduced-fat sour cream**
- **1 tablespoon fat-free (skim) milk**
- **1 to 1½ teaspoons lemon juice**
- **⅛ teaspoon ground turmeric**
- **1¼ cups hot cooked broccoli florets**

Combine all ingredients except broccoli in top of double boiler. Cook over simmering water 5 minutes or until heated through, stirring constantly. Serve over hot cooked broccoli.

Nutrients per Serving: Calories 44; Total Fat 1g; Saturated Fat <1g; Protein 2g; Total Carbohydrates 7g; Fiber 2g; Cholesterol 4mg; Sodium 216mg

RASPBERRY MANGO SALAD

MAKES 4 SERVINGS ✦ NET CARB COUNT: 2 GRAMS

2   cups arugula

I   cup torn Bibb or Boston lettuce

½   cup watercress, stems removed

I   cup diced mango

¾   cup fresh raspberries

¼   cup (I½ ounces) crumbled blue cheese

I   tablespoon olive oil

I   tablespoon water

I   tablespoon raspberry vinegar

⅛   teaspoon salt

⅛   teaspoon black pepper

I. Combine arugula, lettuce, watercress, mango, raspberries and cheese in medium bowl.

2. Shake remaining ingredients in small jar. Pour over salad; toss to coat. Serve immediately.

Nutrients per Serving: Calories 98; Total Fat 8g; Saturated Fat 3g; Protein 3g; Total Carbohydrates 4g; Fiber 2g; Cholesterol 8mg; Sodium 227mg

COLD ASPARAGUS WITH LEMON-MUSTARD DRESSING

MAKES 2 SERVINGS ✦ NET CARB COUNT: 5 GRAMS

12 **fresh asparagus spears**

 2 **tablespoons fat-free mayonnaise**

 1 **tablespoon sweet brown mustard**

 1 **tablespoon fresh lemon juice**

 1 **teaspoon grated lemon peel, divided**

1. Steam asparagus until crisp-tender and bright green; immediately drain and rinse under cold water. Cover and refrigerate until chilled.

2. Combine mayonnaise, mustard and lemon juice in small bowl; blend well. Stir in ½ teaspoon lemon peel; set aside.

3. Divide asparagus between 2 plates. Spoon 2 tablespoons dressing over top of each serving; sprinkle each with ¼ teaspoon lemon peel. Garnish with carrot strips and edible flowers, such as pansies, violets or nasturtiums, if desired.

Nutrients per Serving (6 spears plus 2 tablespoons dressing): Calories 39; Total Fat 1g; Saturated Fat <1g; Protein 3g; Total Carbohydrates 7g; Fiber 2g; Cholesterol 0; Sodium 294mg

EASY GREEK SALAD

MAKES 6 SERVINGS ✦ NET CARB COUNT: 4 GRAMS

6 leaves Romaine lettuce, torn into 1½-inch pieces

1 cucumber, peeled and sliced

1 tomato, chopped

½ cup sliced red onion

⅓ cup (1 ounce) crumbled feta cheese

2 tablespoons extra-virgin olive oil

2 tablespoons lemon juice

1 teaspoon dried oregano leaves

½ teaspoon salt

1. Combine lettuce, cucumber, tomato, onion and cheese in large serving bowl.

2. Whisk together oil, lemon juice, oregano and salt in small bowl. Pour over lettuce mixture; toss until coated. Serve immediately.

Serving Suggestion: This simple but delicious salad makes a great accompaniment for grilled steaks or chicken.

Nutrients per Serving: Calories 71; Total Fat 6g; Saturated Fat 1g; Protein 1g; Total Carbohydrates 5g; Fiber 1g; Cholesterol 4mg; Sodium 249mg

FAR EAST TABBOULEH

MAKES 4 SERVINGS ✦ NET CARB COUNT: 10 GRAMS

- ¾ **cup uncooked bulgur**
- 1¾ **cups boiling water**
- 2 **tablespoons reduced-sodium teriyaki sauce**
- 2 **tablespoons lemon juice**
- 1 **tablespoon olive oil**
- ¾ **cup diced seeded cucumber**
- ¾ **cup diced seeded tomato**
- ½ **cup thinly sliced green onions**
- ½ **cup minced fresh cilantro or parsley**
- 1 **tablespoon minced fresh ginger**
- 1 **clove garlic, minced**

1. Combine bulgur and water in small bowl. Cover with plastic wrap; let stand 45 minutes or until bulgur is puffed, stirring occasionally. Drain in wire mesh sieve; discard liquid.

2. Combine bulgur, teriyaki sauce, lemon juice and oil in large bowl. Stir in cucumber, tomato, onions, cilantro, ginger and garlic until well blended. Cover; refrigerate 4 hours, stirring occasionally. Garnish as desired.

Nutrients per Serving: Calories 73; Total Fat 2g; Saturated Fat <1g; Protein 2g; Total Carbohydrates 13g; Fiber 3g; Cholesterol 0; Sodium 156mg

SIDES & SALADS

LEMON-GARLIC BROCCOLI OVER SPAGHETTI SQUASH

MAKES 6 SERVINGS ✦ NET CARB COUNT: 11 GRAMS

1	**spaghetti squash (2 pounds)**
1	**can (about 14 ounces) chicken broth**
10	**large cloves garlic, halved**
2	**tablespoons lemon juice**
3	**fresh sage leaves**
2	**cups broccoli florets**

1. Place spaghetti squash in large saucepan. Pierce skin with fork. Add enough water to cover. Bring to a boil over high heat. Reduce heat to low; simmer, covered, 20 to 30 minutes or until squash is soft. Cut squash in half lengthwise; remove seeds. Set aside.

2. Meanwhile, combine broth and garlic in small saucepan. Bring to a boil over high heat. Reduce heat to low; simmer 15 minutes or until tender. Remove from heat; cool slightly.

3. Place broth, garlic, lemon juice and sage in food processor; process until smooth. Return mixture to saucepan; keep warm.

4. Combine broccoli and ¼ cup water in large nonstick skillet with tight-fitting lid. Bring to a boil over high heat. Reduce heat to medium. Cover and steam 5 minutes or until broccoli is crisp-tender.

5. Using fork, remove spaghetti-like strands from squash. Place squash and broccoli in medium bowl; pour lemon-garlic mixture over squash mixture. Mix well. Garnish as desired. Serve immediately.

Nutrients per Serving: Calories 71; Total Fat <1g; Saturated Fat <1g; Protein 4g; Total Carbohydrates 14g; Fiber 3g; Cholesterol 0; Sodium 246mg

MARINATED TOMATO SALAD

MAKES 8 SERVINGS ✦ NET CARB COUNT: 7 GRAMS

Marinade

1½ **cups tarragon or white wine vinegar**

½ **teaspoon salt**

¼ **cup finely chopped shallots**

2 **tablespoons finely chopped chives**

2 **tablespoons fresh lemon juice**

¼ **teaspoon white pepper**

2 **tablespoons extra-virgin olive oil**

Salad

6 **plum tomatoes, quartered vertically**

2 **large yellow tomatoes,* sliced horizontally into ½-inch slices**

16 **red cherry tomatoes, halved vertically**

16 **small yellow pear tomatoes,* halved vertically**

*Substitute 10 plum tomatoes, quartered vertically, for yellow tomatoes and yellow pear tomatoes, if desired.

1. To prepare marinade, combine vinegar and salt in large bowl; stir until salt is completely dissolved. Add shallots, chives, lemon juice and white pepper; mix well. Slowly whisk in oil until well blended.

2. Add tomatoes to marinade; toss well. Cover and let stand at room temperature 2 to 3 hours.

3. To serve, place 3 plum tomato quarters on each of 8 salad plates. Add 2 slices yellow tomato, 4 cherry tomato halves and 4 pear tomato halves. Garnish each plate with sunflower sprouts, if desired. (Or, place all marinated tomatoes on large serving plate.)

Nutrients per Serving: Calories 72; Total Fat 4g; Saturated Fat <1g; Protein 2g; Total Carbohydrates 9g; Fiber 2g; Cholesterol 0; Sodium 163mg

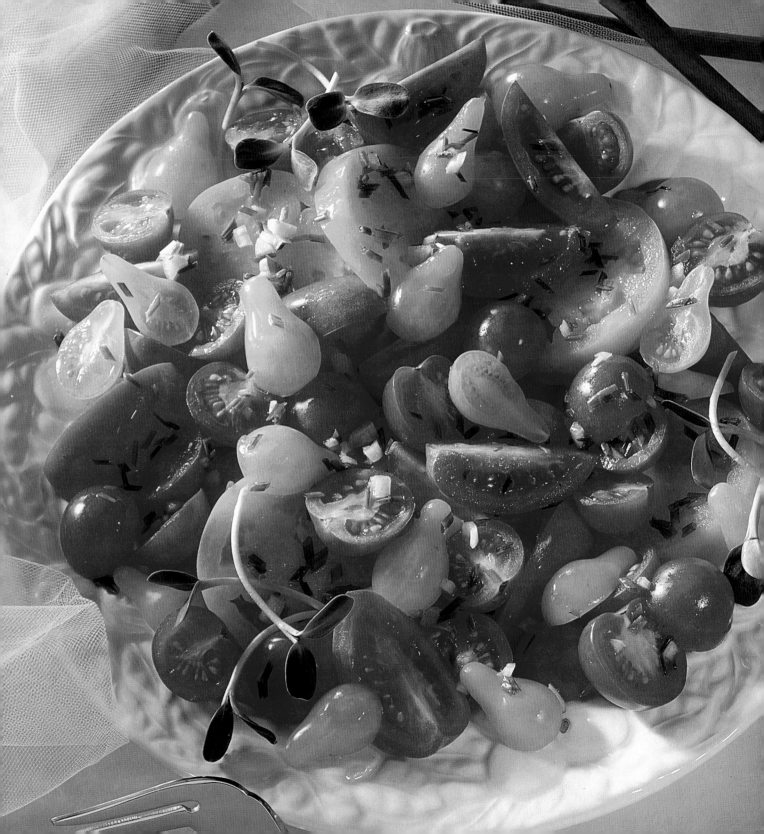

QUICK VEGETABLE & PESTO SALAD

MAKES 6 SERVINGS ✦ NET CARB COUNT: 8 GRAMS

¼ **cup reduced-fat mayonnaise**

¼ **cup refrigerated pesto sauce**

1 **tablespoon balsamic vinegar**

6 **cups assorted fresh vegetables from salad bar, such as sliced mushrooms, shredded carrots, red onion strips, sliced radishes, peas, broccoli florets and bell pepper strips (about 1½ pounds)**

Lettuce leaves

1. Combine mayonnaise, pesto and vinegar in large bowl; stir until well blended.

2. Add vegetables; toss well to coat. Cover and refrigerate 10 minutes. Arrange lettuce leaves on salad plates. Top with vegetable mixture.

Note: Chilling for 30 minutes will improve the flavor of this easy side-dish salad.

Nutrients per Serving (1 cup): Calories 130; Total Fat 8g; Saturated Fat 1g; Protein 4g; Total Carbohydrates 11g; Fiber 3g; Cholesterol 5 mg; Sodium 186mg

SIDES & SALADS

BRAISED ORIENTAL CABBAGE

MAKES 6 SERVINGS ✦ NET CARB COUNT: 5 GRAMS

½ **small head green cabbage (about ½ pound)**

1 **small head bok choy (about ¾ pound)**

½ **cup fat-free reduced-sodium chicken broth**

2 **tablespoons rice wine vinegar**

2 **tablespoons reduced-sodium soy sauce**

1 **tablespoon brown sugar**

¼ **teaspoon red pepper flakes (optional)**

1 **tablespoon water**

1 **tablespoon cornstarch**

1. Cut cabbage into 1-inch pieces. Cut woody stems from bok choy leaves; slice stems into ½-inch pieces. Cut tops of leaves into ½-inch slices; set aside.

2. Combine cabbage and bok choy stems in large nonstick skillet. Add broth, vinegar, soy sauce, brown sugar and red pepper flakes, if desired.

3. Bring to a boil over high heat. Reduce heat to medium. Cover and simmer 5 minutes or until vegetables are crisp-tender.

4. Blend water into cornstarch in small bowl until smooth. Stir into skillet. Cook and stir 1 minute or until sauce boils and thickens.

5. Stir in reserved bok choy leaves; cook 1 minute.

Nutrients per Serving: Calories 34; Total Fat <1g; Saturated Fat <1g; Protein 2g; Total Carbohydrates 6g; Fiber 1g; Cholesterol 0; Sodium 170mg

CHOCOLATE CANNOLI

MAKES 8 SERVINGS ✦ NET CARB COUNT: 11 GRAMS

1	**cup heavy cream**
1	**ounce (1 square) unsweetened chocolate**
⅔	**cup sucralose-based sugar substitute**
⅓	**cup whole milk ricotta cheese**
1	**teaspoon vanilla or almond extract**
¼	**teaspoon salt**
8	**unfilled cannoli shells (½ ounce each)***
1	**teaspoon crushed pistachio nuts (optional)**

*Cannoli shells can be found at Italian bakeries and delis or in ethnic food aisles at some supermarkets. If shells are unavailable, serve filling in dessert dish with sugar wafer or other cookie.

1. In an electric mixer, whip cream until stiff peaks form. Set aside.

2. Place chocolate in small microwavable bowl and microwave at HIGH, stirring at 30-second intervals until chocolate is melted.

3. Combine sugar substitute, ricotta, vanilla and salt in medium bowl. Stir in melted chocolate. Fold reserved whipped cream into mixture.

4. Spoon or pipe ¼ cup mixture into each cannoli shell. Garnish with crushed pistachio nuts, if desired.

Nutrients per Serving (1 cannoli): Calories 230; Total Fat 18g; Saturated Fat 10g; Protein 3g; Total Carbohydrates 12g; Fiber 1g; Cholesterol 46mg; Sodium 23mg

CHOCOLATE FONDUE WITH FRESH FRUIT

MAKES 8 SERVINGS ✦ NET CARB COUNT: 6 GRAMS

3 tablespoons unsweetened cocoa

1 cup heavy cream

4 ounces (½ cup) cream cheese, cut in chunks

3 tablespoons and 1 teaspoon sucralose-based sugar substitute

½ teaspoon vanilla

24 green or red seedless grapes

12 small to medium strawberries, halved, or 6 large strawberries quartered

1. In a small saucepan or fondue pot over low heat, combine the cocoa with ½ cup cream and whisk to mix completely while heating. When cream-cocoa mixture is hot and thick, add remaining cream and the cream cheese and cook, stirring constantly, until mixture is smooth and thick. Add sugar substitute and vanilla, stirring to mix.

2. Transfer mixture to a holder with warmer candle and keep warm over very low heat. Arrange grapes and strawberries on a plate. Provide each guest with a 7-inch long wooden skewer or a fondue fork for dipping.

Tip: Substitute other low-carb fruit in season for the grapes and strawberries.

Nutrients per Serving (6 pieces fruit plus 3 tablespoons fondue): Calories 177; Total Fat 16g; Saturated Fat 10g; Protein 2g; Total Carbohydrates 7g; Fiber 1g; Cholesterol 57mg; Sodium 55mg

DESSERTS

CHOCOLATE PEANUT BUTTER ICE CREAM SANDWICHES

MAKES 4 SERVINGS ✦ NET CARB COUNT: 14 GRAMS

2 tablespoons creamy peanut butter

8 chocolate wafer cookies

⅔ cup no-sugar-added vanilla ice cream, softened

1. Spread peanut butter over flat sides of all cookies

2. Spoon ice cream over peanut butter on 4 cookies. Top with remaining 4 cookies, peanut butter sides down. Press down lightly to force ice cream to edges of sandwich.

3. Wrap each sandwich in foil; seal tightly. Freeze at least 2 hours or up to 5 days.

Nutrients per Serving (1 cookie sandwich): Calories 129; Total Fat 7g; Saturated Fat 3g; Protein 4g; Total Carbohydrates 15g; Fiber 1g; Cholesterol 4mg; Sodium 124mg

PINEAPPLE-GINGER BAVARIAN

MAKES 5 SERVINGS ✦ NET CARB COUNT: 12 GRAMS

1 **can (8 ounces) crushed pineapple in juice, drained and liquid reserved**
1 **package (4 serving size) sugar-free orange gelatin**
1 **cup sugar-free ginger ale**
1 **cup plain nonfat yogurt**
¾ **teaspoon grated fresh ginger**
½ **cup whipping cream**
1 **packet sugar substitute**
¼ **teaspoon vanilla**

1. Combine reserved pineapple juice with enough water to equal ½ cup liquid. Pour into small saucepan. Bring to a boil over high heat.

2. Place gelatin in medium bowl. Add pineapple juice mixture; stir until gelatin is completely dissolved. Add ginger ale and half of crushed pineapple; stir until well blended. Add yogurt; whisk until well blended. Pour into 5 individual ramekins. Cover each ramekin with plastic wrap; refrigerate until firm.

3. Meanwhile, combine remaining half of pineapple with ginger in small bowl. Cover with plastic wrap; refrigerate.

4. Just before serving, beat cream in small deep bowl at high speed of electric mixer until soft peaks form. Add sugar substitute and vanilla; beat until stiff peaks form.

5. To serve, top bavarian with 1 tablespoon whipped topping and 1 tablespoon pineapple mixture.

Tip: To save time, use 2 tablespoons ready-made whipped topping to garnish, if desired.

Nutrients per Serving: Calories 147; Total Fat 9g; Saturated Fat 6g; Protein 4g; Total Carbohydrates 12g; Fiber <1g; Cholesterol 34mg; Sodium 111mg

DESSERTS

COCONUT FLAN

MAKES 4 SERVINGS ✦ NET CARB COUNT: 12 GRAMS

3   **tablespoons water**

1   **envelope unflavored gelatin**

1   **can (14½ ounces) unsweetened coconut milk**

8   **packets sucralose-based sugar substitute**

2   **tablespoons powdered sugar**

½   **teaspoon vanilla**

4   **tablespoons toasted flaked coconut**

2   **(½-inch thick) slices fresh pineapple, cut into bite-size pieces**

1. Place water in small bowl and sprinkle gelatin over top; set aside.

2. Place coconut milk, sugar substitute, powdered sugar and vanilla in medium saucepan. Heat over medium heat, stirring to dissolve sugar and smooth out coconut milk. Do not boil. Add gelatin mixture and stir until gelatin is dissolved.

3. Pour into 4 (5-ounce) custard cups and chill until set, about 3 hours. To unmold, run a thin blade around the outside edge of cups and place bottoms in hot water for about 30 seconds. Place serving plate over cup, invert and shake until flan drops onto plate. Top each flan with 1 tablespoon toasted coconut and arrange ⅓ of pineapple pieces on plate. Refrigerate leftovers promptly and eat within 2 days.

Nutrients per Serving: Calories 261; Total Fat 24g; Saturated Fat 21g; Protein 4g; Total Carbohydrates 13g; Fiber 1g; Cholesterol 0; Sodium 18mg

DESSERTS

WHITE CHOCOLATE PUDDING PARFAITS

MAKES 4 SERVINGS ✦ NET CARB COUNT: 15 GRAMS

1 package (4-serving size) sugar-free instant white chocolate pudding mix

2 cups (low-fat) 2% milk

¾ cup whipping cream

1½ cups fresh raspberries or sliced strawberries

2 tablespoons chopped roasted shelled pistachio nuts or chopped toasted macadamia nuts

1. Add pudding mix to milk; beat with wire whisk or electric mixer 2 minutes. Refrigerate 5 minutes or until thickened. Beat whipping cream in small deep bowl with electric mixer at high speed until stiff peaks form. Fold whipped cream into pudding.

2. In each of 4 parfait or wine glasses, layer ¼ cup pudding and 2 tablespoons raspberries. Repeat layers. Spoon remaining pudding over berries. Serve immediately or cover and chill up to 6 hours before serving. Just before serving, sprinkle with nuts.

Nutrients per Serving: Calories 284; Total Fat 21g; Saturated Fat 12g; Protein 7g; Total Carbohydrates 19g; Fiber 4g; Cholesterol 71mg; Sodium 291mg

EASY RASPBERRY ICE CREAM

MAKES 3 SERVINGS ✦ NET CARB COUNT: 12 GRAMS

8 ounces (1¾ cups) frozen unsweetened raspberries

2 to 3 tablespoons powdered sugar

½ cup whipping cream

1. Place raspberries in food processor fitted with steel blade. Process using on/off pulsing action about 15 seconds or until raspberries resemble coarse crumbs.

2. Add sugar; process using on/off pulsing action until smooth. With processor running, add cream, processing until well blended. Serve immediately.

Variation: Substitute other low-carb fruits such as strawberries for the raspberries.

Nutrients per Serving (½ cup): Calories 193; Total Fat 15g; Saturated Fat 9g; Protein 2g; Total Carbohydrates 15g; Fiber 3g; Cholesterol 54mg; Sodium 15mg

STRAWBERRY-TOPPED CHEESECAKE CUPS

MAKES 8 SERVINGS ✦ NET CARB COUNT: 15 GRAMS

1	**cup sliced strawberries**
10	**packages sugar substitute, divided**
1	**teaspoon vanilla, divided**
½	**teaspoon grated orange peel**
¼	**teaspoon grated fresh ginger**
1	**package (8 ounces) cream cheese, softened**
½	**cup sour cream**
2	**tablespoons granulated sugar**
16	**vanilla wafers, crushed**

1. Combine strawberries, 1 package sugar substitute, ¼ teaspoon vanilla, orange peel and grated ginger in medium bowl; toss gently. Let stand 20 minutes to allow flavors to blend.

2. Meanwhile, combine remaining 9 packets sugar substitute, cream cheese, sour cream and granulated sugar in medium mixing bowl. Add remaining ¾ teaspoon vanilla; beat 30 seconds on low speed of electric mixer. Increase to medium speed; beat 30 seconds or until smooth.

3. Spoon cream cheese mixture into 8 individual ¼-cup ramekins. Top each with about 2 tablespoons vanilla wafer crumbs and about 2 tablespoons strawberry mixture.

Nutrients per Serving: Calories 205; Total Fat 15g; Saturated Fat 9g; Protein 3g; Total Carbohydrates 15g; Fiber <1g; Cholesterol 36mg; Sodium 127mg

SPEEDY PINEAPPLE-LIME SORBET

MAKES 8 SERVINGS ✦ NET CARB COUNT: 15 GRAMS

1 **ripe pineapple, cut into cubes (about 4 cups)**
⅓ **cup frozen limeade concentrate, thawed**
1 **to 2 tablespoons fresh lime juice**
1 **teaspoon grated lime peel**

1. Arrange pineapple in single layer on large baking pan; freeze at least 1 hour or until very firm. (Use metal spatula to transfer pineapple to resealable plastic freezer food storage bags; freeze up to 1 month.)

2. Combine frozen pineapple, limeade concentrate, lime juice and lime peel in food processor; process until smooth and fluffy. If mixture doesn't become smooth and fluffy, let stand 30 minutes to soften slightly; then repeat processing. Garnish as desired. Serve immediately.

Note: This dessert is best if served immediately, but it can be made ahead, stored in the freezer and then softened several minutes before being served.

Nutrients per Serving (½ cup): Calories 56; Total Fat <1g; Saturated Fat <1g; Protein <1g; Total Carbohydrates 15g; Fiber 1g; Cholesterol 0; Sodium 1mg

CHOCOLATE-ALMOND MERINGUE PUFFS

MAKES 15 SERVINGS ✦ NET CARB COUNT: 5 GRAMS

2 **tablespoons granulated sugar**

3 **packets sugar substitute**

1½ **teaspoons unsweetened cocoa powder**

2 **egg whites, room temperature**

½ **teaspoon vanilla**

¼ **teaspoon cream of tartar**

¼ **teaspoon almond extract**

⅛ **teaspoon salt**

1½ **ounces sliced almonds**

3 **tablespoons sugar-free seedless raspberry fruit spread**

1. Preheat oven to 275°F. Combine granulated sugar, sugar substitute and cocoa powder in small bowl; set aside.

2. Place egg whites in small bowl; beat at high speed of electric mixer until foamy. Add vanilla, cream of tartar, almond extract and salt; beat until soft peaks form. Add sugar mixture, 1 tablespoon at a time, beating until stiff peaks form.

3. Line baking sheet with foil. Spoon 15 equal mounds of egg white mixture onto foil. Sprinkle with almonds.

4. Bake 1 hour. Turn oven off but do not open door. Leave puffs in oven 2 hours longer or until completely dry. Remove from oven; cool completely.

5. Stir fruit spread and spoon about ½ teaspoon onto each meringue just before serving.

Tip: Puffs are best if eaten the same day they're made. If necessary, store in airtight container, adding fruit topping at time of serving.

Nutrients per Serving (1 puff): Calories 36; Total Fat 1g; Saturated Fat <1g; Protein 1g; Total Carbohydrates 5g; Fiber <1g; Cholesterol 0; Sodium 27mg

MILK CHOCOLATE FROZEN MOUSSE

MAKES 6 SERVINGS ✦ NET CARB COUNT: 11 GRAMS

1½ **cups heavy cream, divided**

½ **cup water**

1 **envelope unflavored gelatin**

2 **tablespoons unsweetened cocoa**

½ **teaspoon ground cinnamon**

6 **tablespoons powdered sugar**

¼ **teaspoon salt**

2 **tablespoons sucralose-based sugar substitute**

1 **teaspoon vanilla extract**

3 **tablespoons honey-roasted sliced almonds**

1. Combine ½ cup cream and water in small saucepan. Sprinkle on gelatin. Set aside 5 minutes to soften. Stir in cocoa, cinnamon, powdered sugar and salt. Stir over low heat until cocoa is blended and gelatin dissolves. Remove from heat and cool slightly. Stir in sugar substitute and vanilla.

2. Chill gelatin mixture 1 hour or until partially set. Pour remaining 1 cup cream into bowl of electric mixer. Beat to form stiff peaks. Gently fold chocolate mixture into cream. Spoon into 2-quart soufflé or casserole dish. Sprinkle with sliced almonds. Place in freezer 1 hour or until semi-frozen.

Nutrients per Serving (½ cup): Calories 275; Total Fat 25g; Saturated Fat 14g; Protein 3g; Total Carbohydrates 12g; Fiber 1g; Cholesterol 82mg; Sodium 129mg

DESSERTS

INDEX

Apple and Brie Omelet 62

Beef

Blue Cheese-Stuffed Sirloin
Patties 114

Low-Carb Lasagna 120

Sirloin with Sweet Caramelized
Onions 118

Steaks with Zesty Merlot
Sauce 116

Stir-Fry Beef & Vegetable
Soup 96

Blue Cheese-Stuffed Sirloin
Patties 114

Braised Oriental Cabbage 166

Broccoli with Creamy Lemon
Sauce 150

Brunch Eggs Olé 60

Chicken and Turkey

Chunky Chicken and
Vegetable Soup 90

Jerk Wings with Ranch
Dipping Sauce 72

Parmesan Turkey Breast . . 112

Quick Orange Chicken . . . 132

Roast Chicken with
Peppers 110

Roast Turkey Breast with
Spinach-Blue Cheese
Stuffing 128

Spinach, Cheese and
Prosciutto-Stuffed
Chicken Breasts 126

Turkey Ham Quesadillas . . . 88

Chocolate

Chocolate Cannoli 168

Chocolate Fondue with
Fresh Fruit 170

Chocolate Peanut Butter Ice
Cream Sandwiches . . 172

Chocolate-Almond
Meringue Puffs 186

Milk Chocolate Frozen
Mousse 188

White Chocolate Pudding
Parfaits 178

Chocolate Cannoli 168

Chocolate Fondue with Fresh
Fruit 170

Chocolate Peanut Butter Ice
Cream Sandwiches 172

Chocolate-Almond Meringue
Puffs 186

Chunky Chicken and
Vegetable Soup 90

Brunch Eggs Olé 60

Crustless Individual Spinach
 & Bacon Quiche 56

Easy Brunch Frittata 64

Feta Brunch Bake 58

Greek Isles Omelet 66

Ham & Cheddar Frittata . . . 54

Mexican Omelet Roll-Ups
 with Avocado
 Sauce 68

Spicy Crabmeat Frittata . . . 70

Far East Tabbouleh 158

Feta Brunch Bake 58

Fish and Seafood

Cioppino 100

Crab Canapés 78

Grilled Salmon Fillets,
 Asparagus and
 Onions 140

Jicama & Shrimp Cocktail
 with Roasted Red
 Pepper Sauce 82

Mediterranean Shrimp
 Soup 104

Mesquite-Grilled Salmon
 Fillets 136

Pecan Catfish with
 Cranberry
 Compote 130

Smoked Salmon Roses 74

Southern Crab Cakes with
 Rémoulade Dipping
 Sauce 86

Cioppino 100

Coconut Flan 176

Cold Asparagus with
 Lemon Mustard
 Dressing 154

Crab Canapes 78

Crustless Individual Spinach
 & Bacon Quiche 56

Desserts

Chocolate Cannoli 168

Chocolate Fondue with
 Fresh Fruit 170

Chocolate Peanut Butter
 Ice Cream
 Sandwiches 172

Chocolate-Almond
 Meringue Puffs 186

Coconut Flan 176

Easy Raspberry Ice
 Cream 180

Milk Chocolate Frozen
 Mousse 188

Pineapple-Ginger
 Bavarian 174

Speedy Pineapple-Lime
 Sorbet 184

Strawberry-Topped
 Cheesecake Cups . . . 182

White Chocolate Pudding
 Parfaits 178

Easy Brunch Frittata 64

Easy Greek Salad 156

Easy Raspberry Ice
 Cream 180

Eggs

Apple and Brie Omelet . . . 62

INDEX

Spicy Crabmeat
   Frittata 70

Greek Isles Omelet 66

Grilled Pork Tenderloin
   Medallions 134

Grilled Salmon Fillets,
   Asparagus and
   Onions 140

Ham & Cheddar Frittata 54

Ham and Cheese "Sushi" 76

Herbed Stuffed Tomatoes 80

Hot and Sour Soup 102

Indian-Style Vegetable
   Stir-Fry 144

Italian Sausage and Vegetable
   Stew 92

Jerk Wings with Ranch Dipping
   Sauce 72

Jicama & Shrimp Cocktail with
   Roasted Red Pepper
   Sauce 82

Lamb

   Moroccan-Style Lamb
      Chops 138

Lemon-Garlic Broccoli over
   Spaghetti Squash 160

Low-Carb Lasagna 120

Marinated Tomato Salad 162

Mediterranean Shrimp
   Soup 104

Mesquite-Grilled Salmon
   Fillets 136

Mexican Omelet Roll-Ups
   with Avocado Sauce 68

Mexican Tortilla Soup 106

Milk Chocolate Frozen
   Mousse 188

Moroccan-Style Lamb
   Chops 138

Parmesan Turkey Breast 112

Pecan Catfish with Cranberry
   Compote 130

Pineapple-Ginger Bavarian 174

Pork

   Crustless Individual
      Spinach & Bacon
      Quiche 56

   Grilled Pork Tenderloin
      Medallions 134

   Ham & Cheddar Frittata . . . 54

   Ham and Cheese
      "Sushi" 76

   Italian Sausage and
      Vegetable Stew 92

   Pork Kabobs in Margarita
      Marinade 124

Pork Kabobs in Margarita
   Marinade 124

Portobello Mushrooms
   Sesame 84

Pozole 108

Quick Orange Chicken 132

Quick Vegetable &
   Pesto Salad 164

Raspberry Mango Salad 152

Roast Chicken with Peppers . . 110

Roast Turkey Breast with
   Spinach-Blue Cheese
   Stuffing 128

Roasted Red Pepper &
   Tomato Casserole 146

Salads

   Easy Greek Salad 156

   Far East Tabbouleh 158

   Marinated Tomato Salad . . 162

   Quick Vegetable & Pesto
      Salad 164

   Raspberry Mango Salad . . 152

   Santa Fe Grilled Vegetable
      Salad 148

   Sweet-Sour Turnip Green
      Salad 142

Santa Fe Grilled Vegetable
   Salad 148

Sirloin with Sweet
   Caramelized Onions 118

Smoked Salmon Roses 74

Soups

   Chunky Chicken and
      Vegetable Soup 90

Stir-Fry Beef & Vegetable
    Soup 96

Strawberry-Topped Cheesecake
    Cups 182

Sweet-Sour Turnip Green
    Salad 142

Thai Noodle Soup 98

Turkey Ham Quesadillas 88

Vegetables

Braised Oriental
    Cabbage 166

Broccoli with Creamy
    Lemon Sauce 150

Cold Asparagus with
    Lemon Mustard
    Dressing 154

Herbed Stuffed
    Tomatoes 80

Indian-Style Vegetable
    Stir-Fry 144

Lemon-Garlic Broccoli
    over Spaghetti
    Squash 160

Portobello Mushrooms
    Sesame 84

Roasted Red Pepper &
    Tomato Casserole . . . 146

Southwest Spaghetti
    Squash 122

White Chocolate Pudding
    Parfaits 178

Cioppino 100

Hot and Sour Soup 102

Italian Sausage and Vegetable
    Stew 92

Mediterranean Shrimp
    Soup 104

Mexican Tortilla Soup 106

Pozole 108

Spicy Pumpkin Soup with
    Green Chili Swirl 94

Stir-Fry Beef & Vegetable
    Soup 96

Thai Noodle Soup 98

Southern Crab Cakes with
    Rémoulade Dipping
    Sauce 86

Southwest Spaghetti Squash . . 122

Speedy Pineapple-Lime
    Sorbet 184

Spicy Crabmeat Frittata 70

Spicy Pumpkin Soup with
    Green Chili Swirl 94

Spinach, Cheese and
    Prosciutto-Stuffed
    Chicken Breasts 126

Steaks with Zesty Merlot
    Sauce 116